TWICE UPON

INDIA'S FAIRYTALE CRICKET VICTORIES OF 1971

NISHAD PAI VAIDYA AND SACHIN BAJAJ

FOREWORD BY SIR CLIVE LLOYD CBE
CARICATURES BY AUSTIN COUTINHO

Notion Press

No.8, 3rd Cross Street
CIT Colony, Mylapore
Chennai, Tamil Nadu – 600004

First Published by Notion Press 2021
Copyright © Nishad Pai Vaidya and Sachin Bajaj 2021
All Rights Reserved.
Cover design and sketches by Austin Coutinho

ISBN 978-1-63873-520-5

Contents

Foreword

Having watched Indian cricket for decades, I can say that their performances in 1971 marked their ascendancy in Test cricket. Their Test series wins in the Caribbean and England lifted them and gave them the belief that they could beat the best at the highest level. It was a really good contest between India and the West Indies that year. Although we were at the receiving end, it was really good to see Indian cricket finding its strength. The West Indian public also admired them for the way they played their cricket that year.

There are so many highlights for India on that tour, but one man who stood out was Sunil Gavaskar, who was playing his very first Test series. He became their mainstay and kept going from strength to strength. I have always admired Sunny and he is a great friend of mine. What I admired most about him were his powers of concentration. In the years that followed, he became an inspiration for his countrymen, which encouraged someone like a young Sachin Tendulkar.

Dilip Sardesai was someone I knew well and admired as a batsman. He did not quite get the recognition like Sunny but with 642 runs in the Test series, he was just as good. The other Indian batsman I enjoyed watching was Gundappa Viswanath.

When India won the Test match at Trinidad, the charismatic Salim Durani delivered with decisive blows during our second innings, dismissing our captain Sir Garry Sobers and me in quick succession. Durani was a very good cricketer and some even felt he was the Garry Sobers of India

On that tour, India came in with some of the best spinners in the world such as Bishan Singh Bedi, Erapalli Prasanna and S Venkataraghavan. All along, they were very well led by their newly appointed captain Ajit Wadekar. The win in the Caribbean gave India the impetus and they carried all that confidence into the tour to England, where they replicated their success against Ray Illingworth's men. What a year it was for Indian cricket!

I have always had a great affinity with India. In 1966-67, I made my Test debut at Bombay (now Mumbai). Then, in 1974-75, I embarked on my captaincy journey when we visited India – winning my first Test and series as a leader on that trip. During the fifth and final Test of that series, I recorded my highest Test score – 242 not out.

Let me share an anecdote to reveal the kind of bond we shared with the Indian public. The 1974-75 series was a great contest. We had taken a 2-0 lead in the five-match series but India bounced back to level it at 2-2. As we got ready to leave for Bombay for the decider, a holy man was at our hotel. "Mr Lloyd. I know what is going to happen. You will win the toss and then win the match," he proclaimed. That is exactly what happened at Bombay as I won the toss, chose to bat and we scored big to setup a 3-2 series win. Years later, when I returned to the same hotel, I ran into our 'fortune-teller'. "Do you remember me?" he asked. "How can I forget?" I said with a smile. I have always enjoyed contests with India and have shared a warm relationship with its huge cricket loving public.

Today, India are one of the best sides in the world and physically fit to take on the challenge of international cricket. At the time of writing, they have made it to the first ever World Test

Championship final and I expect them to give a good account of themselves.

I would like to wish Nishad and Sachin the very best for this book. I hope it becomes a bestseller and gives people a great insight into cricket from yesteryear.

Sir Clive Lloyd CBE
March 18, 2021

Sir Clive Lloyd CBE represented West Indies in 110 Tests and 87 ODIs. He is best remembered for captaining one of the greatest teams in cricket history. Under his leadership, West Indies dominated Test cricket and also won the first two World Cups.

Acknowledgements

To start off, we would like to thank all the cricketers who made the special year 1971 possible. Up until then, India hadn't tasted much cricketing success but those twin victories in West Indies and England built great confidence. In later years, India achieved glory on the world stage and one may say that it may not have been possible had Ajit Wadekar and his men not broken barriers back in 1971.

A big thank you to Clayton Murzello, Mid-Day's Group Sports Editor, for guiding us through every step in getting this book together. Thanks to his deep knowledge and experience, we were able to peel the layers and unearth numerous incidents and stories from those path-breaking tours. This book would not have been possible without his support and guidance.

The wonderful caricatures for this book were created by Austin Coutinho. Devendra Prabhudesai, noted author who has penned numerous cricketing books, helped us in strategising our research and focus on important details.

We would like to thank Pravin Mahida for proof-reading our whole manuscript and the young Kausthub Gudipati, who documented all the statistics and the scorecards for this book.

We would also like to thank Sidharth Bhatia, the editor of The Wire, for planting the seed of this idea. Ambareesh Chakraborty, an old friend of Sachin's, for giving this book its title.

Finally, a big thank you to our family and friends, who over the years, have 'tolerated' our intense passion for cricket. Not only did they help that passion grow but also supported us when we wanted to channelise it and make a contribution to the cricketing world.

Preface

The year 1971 is remembered as an epochal juncture in Indian history. Post-independence, a young nation was learning to walk on its feet, battling numerous issues left behind by nearly two centuries of colonial rule. As a society, India was diffident, tentative and conservative on the world stage – hoping to make it through to the next day. Survival was perhaps the thought that dominated the psyche. This attitude reflected in most walks of life – including the cricket field – where victory, especially overseas, was perhaps a dream bordering on the impossible. A draw at times was good as a win! However, all that changed in the year 1971 – the turning point in Indian history.

On the geopolitical front, Prime Minister Indira Gandhi was confronted with the massive issue of the incoming refugees from the erstwhile East Pakistan. Sensing trouble on both fronts, she took a brave stand in the eye of the world powers – backing the Bangladeshi freedom struggle. India had managed to win two conflicts against Pakistan since independence, but having its arch rival on both wings was a tricky and draining proposition for the country. Even as the United States backed its ally Pakistan, India stood firm and ultimately, the victory in the conflict helped create the new nation of Bangladesh. It is considered as one of India's finest hours on the world stage.

A similar change was seen on the cricket field, where a 29-year-old Ajit Wadekar was thrust into the job of captaincy early in the year. Taking over from a prince, Mansur Ali Khan Pataudi, Wadekar had his task cut out with two away tours to West Indies and England. West Indies weren't at their strongest or their best then, but India weren't only battling the opposition but also a mindset. On the other hand, England were arguably the best team in the world at the time, having gotten the better of Ashes rivals Australia. For a team that had only won overseas in New Zealand in close to 40 years at the highest level, the expectations were perhaps non-existent.

Wadekar led a side that had a mix of experienced men and some promising youngsters. While Dilip Sardesai helped invigorate India's charge in the West Indies with sterling performances totalling up to 642 runs, Sunil Gavaskar carried the torch forward with his mind-boggling feats in his debut series. If Eknath Solkar took blinders at short-leg, Salim Durani delivered critical blows in the pursuit of victory. Holding on to a 1-0 series lead post the victory at Trinidad, India managed to do the unthinkable – winning the series in the Caribbean! Or so we thought... There was more...

They had beaten West Indies but England were a different proposition. Surely, lightening can't strike twice! However, the gods were smiling upon Wadekar and his men, intervening with showers whenever trouble beckoned. Being lucky is one thing but to capitalise on that moment of fortune requires a sense for the occasion. In came BS Chandrasekhar on the world stage, making a comeback to Test cricket and took six wickets at The Oval to rout out the hosts. India went on to replicate their West Indian triumph on English soil – winning the Test series 1-0. For a young nation's confidence, it was a shot in the arm.

Sporting success often mirrors the society one lives in. At the time, these victories reflected a growing confidence of a young nation on the world stage. The hangovers of the past were behind them as they promised to surge ahead with more confidence. In the years ahead, Gavaskar led the charge and others rallied around him. The baton passed on to other big names much later such as Sachin Tendulkar and Virat Kohli – who only built on those successes. India may have won the 1983 and 2011 World Cups, sealed the 1985 World Championship Down Under, clinched the 2007 World T20 among many other significant achievements but 1971 is where it all started.

As we complete 50 years since 1971, this book presents to you 71 anecdotes from those two tours. These stories are put together to make you smile and enjoy a quick cricketing read, but also appreciate the challenges Wadekar and his men went through to set the foundation of success for Indian cricket. It is to remember and thank them for their contribution to Indian cricket.

Nishad Pai Vaidya
Sachin Bajaj
February 2021

Tiger Predicts a Better Tour in 1971

When India played its inaugural Test in 1932 at Lord's, the Col CK Nayudu-led side did its reputation no harm. Up against a team featuring the likes of Douglas Jardine, Frank Woolley, Herbert Sutcliffe, Bill Voce and Wally Hammond to name a few, the Indians fought hard in a 158-run defeat. Mohammad Nissar and Amar Singh in particular had made waves with their pace on Day One, reducing the hosts to 19 for three. Hammond spoke in glowing terms of Amar Singh, likening his pace to "the crack of doom".

However, in the years that followed, tours to England were often forgettable. From the infamous visit in 1936, where captain Maharajkumar of Vizianagram aka Vizzy's whims and fancies took precedence over the team's interests, to the ignominy of being reduced to zero for four in 1952, India struggled in England barring a few bright performances.

In 1967, Mansur Ali Khan Pataudi (nicknamed Tiger) captained the Indian team on their visit to England – emulating his father – who had the same honour in 1946. While India may have lost the Test series 3-0 on that visit under Tiger's leadership, he was optimistic about the future. "Meanwhile, one of our biggest problems being foreign exchange, it would seem good sense to start concentrating on improving our performances abroad. The

1967 England tour was a beginning. Next time we'll be better," he wrote in his book[1]. The following year in 1968, they registered their first ever overseas Test series win, beating New Zealand 3-1.

While Pataudi was confident of a better performance, he may not have envisioned India winning in both West Indies and England. India had their task cut out ahead of the 1971 away tours. In the West Indies, they had lost six out of 10 Tests across two tours – which included a 5-0 drubbing on their previous visit in 1962. In England, they had been beaten in 15 out of 19 appearances – having lost eight on the trot since 1959.

These numbers put into perspective the magnitude of Ajit Wadekar and his team's achievements in 1971.

---

1   Mansur Ali Khan Pataudi, Tiger's Tale – The Story of the Nawab of Pataudi, Publisher – Stanley Paul, London, 1969

Vijay Merchant Picks Sunil Gavaskar for Success

In 1970-71, Sunil Gavaskar announced himself with a good performance for Bombay (now Mumbai) in the Ranji Trophy. With the twin tours ahead, the young opening batsman was in the hunt for a spot in the Indian team. In that endeavour, he had done well enough to impress the man who mattered – Vijay Merchant, the chairman of selectors. Merchant, who was considered as the patriarch of the Indian batting lineage, had singled out Gavaskar as one with great potential.

The former India Test cricketer, Rusi Modi, wrote in 1971, "As far back as September 1969, Vijay Merchant had told me that Gavaskar is the best opening batsman in the country.[2]" This at a time when Gavaskar had played only a handful of First-Class games and wasn't a fixture in the formidable Bombay side. In fact, Gavaskar was still playing Universities cricket. "In a manner of speaking, Gavaskar is Merchant's discovery," Modi wrote.

In fact, when Merchant met the Indian team before its departure for the West Indies, he earmarked Gavaskar as someone the others in the team could emulate. "Though he is the youngest player in the team, the senior players would do well to follow

---

2   Rusi Modi, Sportsweek, April 25, 1971, p. 5

his example," Merchant said in front of the team[3]. Coming from someone of Merchant's stature, that too for a batsman who was yet to play a Test match, it was rich praise for Gavaskar. As it turned out, Gavaskar not only lived up to it on the tour but ended his career 16 years later as a true legend of Indian cricket.

Merchant though shied away from claiming Gavaskar as his discovery. "I am a servant of Indian cricket, not its master," he said after Gavaskar found success in the Caribbean[4].

3   Sunil Gavaskar, Sunny Days, p. 29, Published by Rupa and Co. Nineteenth Impression 2005

4   Khalid A-H Ansari – Interview with Merchant, Sportsweek, May 2, 1971, p. 32

Wadekar Asks Pataudi to Help Him Retain His Spot

As India prepared for a packed schedule in 1971 with the twin tours of West Indies and England in the offing, there was some suspense over captaincy. Mansur Ali Khan Pataudi, the incumbent, was on shaky ground and there was also a possibility of Chandu Borde, his deputy for a major part of the 1960s, taking over. Meanwhile, blissfully unaware that his fortunes would change, Ajit Wadekar was more worried about his spot in the Indian team. In 1970-71, he hadn't had the best of Ranji Trophy campaigns but had managed a big century in the Irani Trophy.

Ahead of the selection meeting, Wadekar and Pataudi practiced at the Brabourne Stadium, where the former asked the latter to ensure his selection for the West Indies tour should he remain captain. On the day the selectors announced the change in captaincy, Wadekar had gone shopping with his wife Rekha. On his return home, he was accosted by a crowd assembled in front of his apartment at the State Bank of India employees' quarters. Initially, he suspected a colleague may have won a promotion[5]. Instead, he was informed of his own promotion on the big stage – taking over the Indian captaincy from Pataudi. The residents of the quarters celebrated the occasion by garlanding

---

5   Ajit Wadekar – as told to H Natarajan – Wisden.com 2002. Accessed at: https://www.espncricinfo.com/story/hey-garry-you-have-to-follow-on-244928

the new Indian captain and distributing sweets. From being a little jittery about his own spot, the left-hander was now thrust into the big job.

"Pataudi took the change in his stride and, when I asked if he was available to play under me, promptly said 'yes'. As for me, I assured Pataudi he would be in my side, which was to be picked the next day," Wadekar recalled[6].

However, Pataudi withdrew from the tour soon after for personal reasons. He only returned to the Indian team to play under Wadekar when England toured India in 1972-73.

---

6   Lokendra Pratap Sahi, Of Wadekar's Curtains and Merchant's Casting Vote, Published on: 06.03.2003. Accessed at: https://www.telegraphindia.com/sports/of-wadekar-s-curtains-and-merchant-s-casting-vote/cid/802995

Pataudi Loses Captaincy to Wadekar

Mansur Ali Khan Pataudi had been thrust into the Indian captaincy during a very tumultuous time. The Indians were in the Caribbean taking on the might of Frank Worrell's men. Pataudi, then aged only 21, was asked to take over the mantle of leadership in the hour of crisis. While that Caribbean sojourn was forgettable, Pataudi built an Indian team over the next few years, backed the spinners and brought in a sense of 'Indianness' to a team that was normally divided on regional lines. However, by 1971, the chairman of selectors, Vijay Merchant was one of those who felt a change in guard was the need of the hour.

During the vital meeting to pick the captain ahead of the back-to-back tours to West Indies and England, the selectors were split over the captaincy issue. As chairman, Merchant used his casting vote to usher in the Wadekar era. The biggest talking point was the absence of Datta Ray, the East Zone selector, who had reportedly resigned in September 1970, and who's status in the panel remained clouded[7]. Had he been present at the meeting, he was expected to back Pataudi – which would have helped him retain the leadership.

---

7   Sportsweek, May 2, 1971

During his time away from the Indian team, Pataudi contested in the general elections held in March 1971. However, he was soundly beaten by Congress's Tayyab Husain[8], who clinched the Gurgaon constituency. In late 1971, Pataudi returned to the cricket field, turning up for Hyderabad in the Ranji Trophy.

---

8   Aniruddha Ghoshal, Beleaguered Congress may field Sharmila Tagore from Gurgaon. Financial Express. Accessed at: https://www.financialexpress.com/archive/beleaguered-congress-may-field-sharmila-tagore-from-gurgaon/1228313/

Vijay Merchant was one of India's greatest batsmen during its early years in Test cricket. His First-Class average of 71.64 is only behind the great Sir Don Bradman's 95.14. In 1971, he was the chairman of selectors, taking the call of appointing Ajit Wadekar as captain.

Selection Shenanigans

Ahead of India's twin tours to West Indies and England in 1971, it was announced that only those players who had featured in Indian domestic cricket in the 1970-71 season would be considered for selection. As a result, Farokh Engineer was ruled out of contention and that opened up a spot for wicketkeepers. The search for the stumper resulted in interesting incidents ahead of the Duleep Trophy final between South Zone and East Zone at the Brabourne Stadium in January 1971, with the chairman of selectors, Vijay Merchant, at the centre of it all.

Daljit Singh, the Bihar wicketkeeper, was the designated stumper for East Zone having donned the gloves in the semi-final. However, minutes before the toss, it is said that Merchant called for East's captain Ramesh Saxena and asked him to field Bengal's Rusi Jeejeebhoy as a wicketkeeper, as they wanted to have a look at him. Saxena gave in and Daljit played on as a batsman. Jeejeebhoy did not set the world alight but found himself on the flight to the Caribbean. Daljit, who was said to be a contender, missed out and never played for India[9].

On the other side, South Zone's manager, PR Man Singh was told by Merchant to let the young Syed Kirmani 'keep instead of Pochiah Krishnamurthy. Instead of following Merchant's word, Man Singh turned towards the South Zone selector, CD Gopinath.

9   Clayton Murzello, Mid-Day, Published on: June 25, 2020. Accessed at - https://
     www.pressreader.com/india/mid-day/20200625/281895890507668

"Play the best 'keeper," were Gopinath's firm instructions[10]. Krishnamurthy retained his place as a wicketkeeper and also won a spot in the Indian team. The young Kirmani had to wait for the England tour later in the year to travel with the Indian team.

However, in an interview, Merchant claims he never asked Saxena to make a change to the line-up and that it was the East Zone captain who asked him if the selectors would like to have a look at Jeejeebhoy. "I said, 'Yes the selectors would like to see a new face but they would not like you to weaken your team thereby in case you wish to include another batsman'," Merchant claimed to have told Saxena[11].

The other interesting fact is that S Venkataraghavan was named captain of the South Zone team before the season, ahead of ML Jaisimha. It is said he was handed the responsibility keeping in mind India's leadership demands. Venkataraghavan was eventually named deputy to Ajit Wadekar for the tour to the West Indies. Interestingly, Jaisimha too made the cut[12].

10 PR Man Singh, Cricket Biryani – The History of Hyderabad Cricket – p 160, Published by Theodore Braganza of The Marine Sports, 2008

11 Khalid A-H Ansari, Interview with Merchant, Sportsweek, May 2, 1971

12 EAS Prasanna, One More Over – An Autobiography, p. 27-28, Published by Roopa and Co. 1978

Wadekar Backs Sardesai in Selection Meeting

As a chairman of selectors, Vijay Merchant was big on his policy of backing youth. During the 1969-70 home season, which featured Test matches against Australia and New Zealand, India handed as many as eight new Test caps. The axing of Mansur Ali Khan Pataudi from captaincy was more evidence of Merchant's plans to usher in a fresh start. However, the new captain, Ajit Wadekar, was firm on one inclusion. Dilip Sardesai, his Bombay teammate, was his trusted lieutenant and Wadekar wanted his stabilising presence in the West Indies.

Up until then, the 30-year-old Sardesai had played 21 Tests for India but hadn't been a breakout star. In those 21 Tests, he had scored 1,190 runs at an average of 33.05 with two centuries and seven fifties. The two centuries, one of them being a double, had come in back-to-back matches against New Zealand in 1965. In six Test appearances thereafter, he had failed to cross 30 in any innings. During the home season in 1969-70, he played the lone Test against Australia at his home ground, Brabourne Stadium. While he was fairly consistent in domestic cricket, his returns during the 1970-71 season weren't very promising.

Despite that, Wadekar had great faith in Sardesai and backed his case in front of the selectors. The Merchant-led committee gave in to the new captain's suggestions to include Sardesai on the flight to the Caribbean[13].

"I am really happy and honoured to lead the Indian team on the forthcoming tour to the West Indies. I am also very grateful to the national selectors for giving me the team which I wanted," Wadekar said in an interview[14] during India's preparatory camp at the Brabourne Stadium.

Sardesai was destined to be a catalyst for India on the tour to West Indies, setting the wheels rolling towards history.

13   Anindya Dutta, The Greatest Year – The 1971 Tours of West Indies and England, Published By Westland Publications Private Limited 2020

14   Jai Galagali's YouTube Channel Accessed at: https://www.youtube.com/ watch?v=Il0nAqifu-c (At 04:05)

Vijay Merchant's Birthday Gift to Kenia Jayantilal

Kenia Jayantilal hit a sparkling century for South Zone during the Duleep Trophy semi-final against West Zone at the Brabourne Stadium in the first week of the year 1971. Watching from the boundary, Vijay Merchant, the chairman of selectors was impressed by what he saw from the Hyderabad opener. In an innings of 134, which featured 21 boundaries, Jayantilal took on Bombay's UK-import Saeed Ahmed Hatteea – who was considered a genuinely quick bowler. The importance of Jayantilal's innings reflects in the fact that the second highest score in the whole game was 62 by PK Belliappa.

"When I went for batting, every third or fourth ball was a bouncer (from Hatteea) and I used to hit from mid-on to fine-leg," Jayantilal recalled. South's first innings lead was enough to take them through to the final against East Zone at the same ground a few days later. It was during this game that there were numerous incidents in the backdrop as the selectors wanted to have a good look at the players before picking the side for the tour to the West Indies.

While Jayantilal did not get a big score in a 10-wicket victory for South, he had done enough to catch the eye of Merchant. "After the selection, he (Merchant) came down and told me – 'I am giving you a birthday gift that you are selected into the Indian team. Good luck. Do well'," Jayantilal recalled[15].

The Duleep Trophy final got over on January 12, a day before Jayantilal celebrated his 23rd birthday. It was surely the greatest birthday gift the young Hyderabadi batsman had received until then.

---

15 Conversation with the author

Timely Action Saves Sunil Gavaskar's Finger

As the Indian team geared up for the tour to the West Indies ahead of their departure, Sunil Gavaskar was asked to avoid batting in the nets by a doctor mid-way through the preparatory camp at the Brabourne Stadium. This was because of a painful whitlow in the middle finger of his left hand. Instead, Gavaskar bowled in the nets and worked on his fitness[16]. The pain aggravated by the time the team were flying from London to New York. A few self-medication techniques and the cold weather during the break at London had an adverse impact on the finger.

Upon landing in New York, it was clear that the youngster needed medical attention. The manager Keki Tarapore took him to the hospital right away. By then, the finger was in bad shape and the doctor quickly performed a short surgical procedure. "Thank God you've come now. If you had delayed by 24 hours, gangrene would have set in and the finger would have to be chopped off," the doctor told a relieved Gavaskar[17]. The timely action saved Gavaskar from catastrophic damage and the only little issue was a few weeks away from the game. He missed out on the initial few games on the trip, which included the first Test at Jamaica.

---

16   Devendra Prabhudesai, SMG – A Biography of Sunil Manohar Gavaskar – Chapter – Bradmanesque Beginning. Published by Rupa and Co 2009
17   Sunil Gavaskar, Sunny Days – Sunil Gavaskar's Own Story p 28-30, Published by Rupa and Co. Nineteenth Impression 2005

One can only imagine the course of history had the worst happened. Fortunately, there was some power looking after the young batsman who was on his way to great things. World cricket was destined to witness the greatness of Gavaskar!

India Miss Connecting Flight and Lose Kit-Bags

India had made the long arduous journey to Jamaica with multiple stopovers and had arrived a day later than expected. En route to Jamaica, the team had missed a connecting flight from New York[18]. What compounded matters was the fact that some of their kit and equipment hadn't boarded the flight along with them. This was a day before they were scheduled to play Jamaica at the Sabina Park, Kingston.

Manager Keki Tarapore then swung into action and used all his skills to ensure that the bags were not only traced but also delivered to the team. However, the team was handicapped without the equipment and Tarapore then dug into his pocket to find a solution. "Without much ado, he also sanctioned us extra money out of his account to buy the kit that was badly needed for our practice, not to speak of the flannels and other apparel which did not measure up to standard," Ajit Wadekar said[19].

On Day One of their first game against Jamaica, India managed to put up a fight thanks to important knocks by Wadekar (70) and Dilip Sardesai (97). The tour opener was a drawn affair with Salim Durani shining in the second innings with an innings of 131.

---

18   Sunder Rajan, India vs West Indies 1971 p. 6. Published by Jaico Publishing House 1971

19   My Cricketing Years, Ajit Wadekar as told to KN Prabhu, p. 15. Published by Vikas Publishing House Pvt Ltd 1973

Viswanath's Injury Paves the Way for Sardesai

Gundappa Viswanath was one of India's best young batsmen heading into the tour to the West Indies. In 1969, the diminutive Karnataka batsman had announced himself with a century on debut against Bill Lawry's Australia at Kanpur. However, Viswanath carried an injury when he boarded the flight to the Caribbean and that ruled him out of the first few games of the tour.

Captain Ajit Wadekar had backed Dilip Sardesai's selection into the squad but it was Viswanath's injury that opened the door for the Bombay batsman. India's opening match of the tour was a First-Class encounter against Jamaica and Sardesai lived up to his captain's faith with an important innings of 97. "But for the fact that he (Viswanath) was unfit, I wouldn't have played the first match of the 1970-71 tour against Jamaica. And if I hadn't played that first match I wouldn't have hit the 97 I did in that game," Sardesai said[20].

Sardesai walked in when India were 17 for two batting first and struck an important 140-run stand with his captain. That innings put the Bombay batsman in the zone and he held on to his spot for the first Test at Jamaica.

---

20 Dilip Sardesai, How We Broke Through In '71, The Illustrated Weekly of India, Vol C, June 10-16, 1979, p. 32-33

Wadekar Keeps Dowe at Bay Despite an Injured Hand

Back in 1962, India were blown away by the West Indies 5-0 in the Test series. The enduring memories of the tour included facing the likes of Wes Hall and Charlie Griffith. Though Griffith did not feature in the Tests, he left a scar on the Indian mindset when he felled the captain Nari Contractor with a blow to the head during a tour game. The impact of that tour lived on in the Indian psyche as they landed in the Caribbean nine years later. The new captain, Ajit Wadekar was determined to bury the psychological scars of the past and decided to lead by example.

India's first fixture of the tour was against Jamaica at Kingston and they were up against Uton Dowe, a young fast bowler who was tipped to carry forward the West Indian legacy. Early in his innings, Wadekar was hit on the hand by Dowe, which tore a blood vessel. Instead of walking back to the dressing room, it was time to show courage and make a statement. Wadekar wanted his batsmen to believe that they had the goods to not only face the fastest bowlers but also score runs off them.

"When I was hit, I knew it was bleeding a bit, but I was sure it wasn't a fracture. I didn't take my gloves off because if I had seen the blood, it would have weakened me," Wadekar reminisced years later[21].

The doughty Indian captain did not flinch and carried on batting for nearly four hours to stitch together a fighting 70, setting the tone for the rest of the tour.

---

21 When Ajit Wadekar Reminisced The Summer of '71. BCCI Official Website. Published on August 16, 2018. Accessed at: https://www.bcci.tv/articles/2018/ news/99893/when-ajit-wadekar-reminisced-the-summer-of-71

From being jittery about his spot to leading the team... The newly appointed captain **Ajit Wadekar** led India to history in 1971.

Jamaica vs Indians – India tour of West Indies 1971 - Tour Match

Dates: 5-8 February 1971 (4-day First-Class match)
Venue: Sabina Park, Kingston, Jamaica
Toss: India, chose to bat
Scores: Indians 272 & 290/7d, Jamaica 280 & 103/1
Result: Draw

INDIANS	FIRST INNINGS		SECOND INNINGS	
A Mankad	b Dowe	3	lbw b Dowe	0
K Jayantilal	c Lewis b Haye	0	c McMorris b Barrett	27
A Wadekar(c)	c & b Barrett	70	lbw b Miles	54
D Sardesai	run out	97	c McMorris b Barrett	3
M Jaisimha	c Lewis b Barrett	15	b Miles	3
S Durani	b Foster	34	c McMorris b Foster	131
S Venkataraghavan	c Lewis b Foster	31	not out	42
P Krishnamurthy†	c Lewis b Foster	1	lbw b Miles	19
D Govindraj	c Wellington b Barrett	13		
E Prasanna	c Lewis b Foster	0		
B Bedi	not out	0		
Extras	(b 1, lb 2, nb 5)	8	(b 9, nb 2)	11
Team Score		272		290/7d

Fall of wickets 1st innings: 1-2, 2-17, 3-157, 4-187, 5-194, 6-255, 7-257, 8-268, 9-272, 10-272

Fall of wickets 2nd innings: 1-0, 2-66, 3-84, 4-125, 5-209, 6-250, 7-290

Bowling figures	O	M	R	W	O	M	R	W
U Dowe	24	2	76	1	20	1	74	1
W Haye	11	2	28	1	13	0	38	0
M Foster	16	8	23	4	24	4	43	1
A Barrett	28.2	4	81	3	16	6	54	2
L Wellington	5	1	14	0	8	2	21	0
O Miles	14	3	42	0	30.1	9	49	3

JAMAICA	FIRST INNINGS		SECOND INNINGS	
S Morgan	lbw b Govindraj	13	lbw b Bedi	14
D Lewis†	b Venkataraghavan	96	not out	67
L Rowe	c Venkataraghavan b Prasanna	19	not out	19
M Foster	run out	0		
E McMorris(c)	c Jayantilal b Prasanna	4		
R Pinnock	c sub b Venkataraghavan	50		
L Wellington	c & b Bedi	5		
A Barrett	c Durani b Bedi	22		
W Haye	run out	60		
O Miles	c Govindraj b Bedi	2		
U Dowe	not out	0		
Extras	(b 4, lb 5)	9	(lb 2, w 1)	3
Team Score		280		103/1

Fall of wickets 1st innings: 1-38, 2-73, 3-78, 4-83, 5-188, 6-189, 7-199, 8-276, 9-280, 10-280

Fall of wickets 2nd innings: 1-53

Bowling figures	O	M	R	W	O	M	R	W
D Govindraj	15	1	61	1	6	0	23	0
M Jaisimha	6	0	28	0	10	2	21	0
B Bedi	33.4	13	58	3	14	5	20	1
E Prasanna	24	10	56	2				
S Venkataraghavan	26	7	61	2	10	4	26	0
S Durani	6	1	7	0				
A Mankad	4	0	10	0				

Note: All scorecards and tour statistics in this book were curated by Kausthub Gudipati

Wadekar Reprimands Solkar and Gavaskar

Ajit Wadekar was just shy of turning 30 when he was handed the task of leading the Indian team on the tour to the West Indies in 1971. While the team had numerous youngsters, it also had some seasoned campaigners. The likes of Salim Durani, S Venkataraghavan, Dilip Sardesai, ML Jaisimha and Erapalli Prasanna had played for India before Wadekar. Sunil Gavaskar, Eknath Solkar, Gundappa Viswanath and Kenia Jayantilal to name a few were the youngsters. In this curious mix, the leader in Wadekar sought to establish some order and discipline.

"There were many senior players. I was a new captain and how was I to tell them something," Wadekar said. Gavaskar and Solkar, the two youngsters and Wadekar's Bombay teammates, were close to their captain. The duo used to make it to the team meetings five minutes ahead of the scheduled time. However, Wadekar would ask one of them to leave and come a little later. Once either of Gavaskar or Solkar returned as instructed, the rest of the team had assembled. Captain Wadekar would then reprimand them by saying, "So late. What is this?"

"After that, everyone started making it (to the team meeting) on time," Wadekar recalled[22]. Talk about 'making an example' out of someone.

---

22 Tribute to Eknath Solkar, Dwarkanath Sanzgiri's YouTube Channel. Accessed at: https://www.youtube.com/watch?v=c1lOmxo0_SM (Starting from 5:10)

West Indies Board President's XI vs Indians – India tour of West Indies 1971 – Tour Match

Dates: 11-14 February 1971 (4-day First-Class match)
Venue: Jarrett Park, Montego Bay, Jamaica
Toss: West Indies Board President's XI, chose to field
Scores: Indians 280 & 172/7d, West Indies Board President's XI 184 & 212/4
Result: Draw

INDIANS	FIRST INNINGS		SECOND INNINGS	
A Mankad	c Camacho b Barrett	47	lbw b Shillingford	1
K Jayantilal	b Julien	33	not out	58
A Wadekar(c)	c Lewis b Barrett	3	c Lewis b Shillingford	28
D Sardesai	run out	24	lbw b Shillingford	25
M Jaisimha	run out	47	b Boyce	11
S Durani	c & b Julien	8	c Camacho b Boyce	7
E Solkar	c & b Barrett	51	run out	6
S Abid Ali	not out	37	b Julien	23
S Venkataraghavan	lbw b Foster	10		
B Bedi	lbw b Foster	0		
R Jeejeebhoy†	b Foster	0		
Extras	(b 5, lb 7, nb 8)	20	(b 4, lb 4, nb 5)	13
Team Score		280		172/7d

Fall of wickets 1st innings: 1-50, 2-58, 3-112, 4-113, 5-148, 6-176, 7-253, 8-280, 9-280, 10-280

Fall of wickets 2nd innings: 1-1, 2-59, 3-87, 4-105, 5-123, 6-136, 7-172

Bowling figures	O	M	R	W	O	M	R	W
K Boyce	21	6	52	0	13	5	19	2
G Shillingford	17	3	45	0	13	2	41	3
B Julien	26	8	41	2	11.5	3	20	1
A Barrett	36	5	90	3	9	2	38	0
M Foster	15.5	4	27	3	16	3	41	0
A Kallicharran	1	0	5	0				

WEST INDIES BOARD PRESIDENT'S XI	FIRST INNINGS		SECOND INNINGS	
S Camacho(c)	run out	39	b Bedi	45
V Amory	b Bedi	40	c Jeejeebhoy b Abid Ali	26
L Rowe	c Jaisimha b Venkataraghavan	23	c Wadekar b Venkataraghavan	27
M Foster	c Abid Ali b Bedi	2	run out	48
A Kallicharran	c Wadekar b Venkataraghavan	6	not out	57
R de Souza	b Bedi	9	not out	2
B Julien	b Venkataraghavan	3		
K Boyce	c Abid Ali b Bedi	41		
A Barrett	c Durrani b Bedi	12		
A Lewis†	not out	5		
G Shillingford	c Jeejeebhoy b Venkataraghavan	1		
Extras	(lb 1, nb 2)	3	(b 5, lb 1, nb 1)	7
Team Score		184		212/4

Fall of wickets 1st innings: 1-72, 2-85, 3-91, 4-102, 5-121, 6-121, 7-128, 8-174, 9-183, 10-184

Fall of wickets 2nd innings: 1-52, 2-99, 3-99, 4-198

Bowling figures	O	M	R	W	O	M	R	W
S Abid Ali	9	2	14	0	6	1	29	1
E Solkar	6	2	9	0	6	0	34	0
B Bedi	32	8	94	5	17	3	58	1
S Venkataraghavan	29.4	9	64	4	18	5	36	1
S Durani	9	1	26	0				
M Jaisimha	4	0	19	0				
A Mankad	2	1	3	0				

Gavaskar and Viswanath Make an Appearance

Sunil Gavaskar and Gundappa Viswanath, India's two promising young batsmen in 1971, had to miss out on the opening Test at Jamaica due to their injuries. While Viswanath was recovering from his knee injury, Gavaskar was recuperating following his surgical procedure on his finger. However, the duo made an appearance in a side-game before the first Test and made an instant impression on the Caribbean public.

India faced the University of West Indies in a 45-over contest at Jamaica. Limited-overs cricket wasn't taken very seriously back then, much like T20 cricket was approached in its early days. Gavaskar opened the batting for the tourists and hit a well-paced 71 to top-score. Batting at No. 3, Viswanath also contributed with 40. They added 77 runs in tandem for the second wicket. Dilip Sardesai continued his positive build-up to the first Test with an innings of 55 as India racked up 255[23].

ML Jaisimha took four wickets as India defended the total with ease. While it was against a lightweight opposition, India had a good work-out but greater challenges lay ahead – which they were destined to overcome with flying colours.

---

23 Sunder Rajan, India vs West Indies 1971 p. 18. Published by Jaico Publishing House 1971

University of West Indies vs Indians – India tour of West Indies 1971 - Tour Match

Date: 16 February 1971 (45-over match)
Venue: Sir Frank Worrell Cricket Ground, Mona, Jamaica
Toss: India, chose to bat
Scores: Indians 255/6 & University of West Indies 154/9
Result: Indians won by 101 runs

INDIANS INNINGS

S Abid Ali	c Hunte b Ramnarace	38
S Gavaskar	c Hutchinson b Ramnarace	71
G Viswanth	c Dougan b Greenidge	40
D Sardesai	c Lewis b Hunte	55
S Durani	run out	17
M Jaisimha	c Greenidge b Hunte	18
E Solkar	not out	12
S Venkataraghavan(c)	not out	2
Extras	(nb 1, w 1)	2
Team Score		255/6 (45 overs)

Did not bat – R Jeejeebhoy, P Krishnamurthy†, D Govindraj

Fall of wickets 1-64, 2-141, 3-171, 4-212, 5-228, 6-253

Bowling figures	O	M	R	W
P Roberts	3	0	22	0
R Greenidge	7	0	44	1
A Hunte	13	1	62	2
K Ramnarace	14	0	67	2
E Lewis	1	0	12	0
E Hammond	7	0	46	0

UNIVERSITY OF WEST INDIES INNINGS

W Clarke	lbw b Abid Ali	5
V Amory	c Venkataraghavan b Jaisimha	38
R Ishmael	c Viswanath b Solkar	4
E Lewis(c)	b Govindraj	0
A Hunte	st Krishnamurthy b Jaisimha	10
H Dougan†	st Krishnamurthy b Sardesai	29
V Hutchinson	c Jaisimha b Venkataraghavan	20
K Ramnarace	not out	22
E Hammond	c Durani b Jaisimha	4
R Greenidge	b Jaisimha	11
P Roberts	not out	0
Extras	(b 4, lb 6, nb 1)	11
Team Score		154/9 (45 overs)

Fall of wickets 1-7, 2-19, 3-20, 4-53, 5-71, 6-108, 7-123, 8-128, 9-150

Bowling figures	O	M	R	W
D Govindraj	6	1	16	1
S Abid Ali	2	0	10	1
E Solkar	6	2	8	1
M Jaisimha	15	1	66	4
S Durani	5	0	19	0
D Sardesai	3	1	2	1
S Gavaskar	2	0	5	0
S Venkataraghavan	6	2	17	1

Sardesai Dismisses the West Indies Fast Bowling

Dilip Sardesai had toured the West Indies in 1962 and had faced the might of the likes of Wes Hall and Charlie Griffith. When India landed in the West Indies in 1971, there were a few hangovers from the previous tour, although the pace attack wasn't as potent as the one from 1962. While Ajit Wadekar set the tone by example, standing tall to Uton Dowe in the first tour game, it was Sardesai who led from the front in the Tests and inspired confidence in his teammates. It wasn't with the bat alone, but Sardesai was dismissive of the bowling even before he'd taken strike in the first Test at Kingston.

As India were put in to bat at Kingston, Kenia Jayantilal and S Abid Ali walked out to face Vanburn Holder and Grayson Shillingford. From the pavillion placed square off the wicket, the rest of the team watched as the West Indian fast bowlers ran in to bowl to the Indian openers. "It was a shiny Sabina Park pitch and the ball was banged in by the bowlers. The wicketkeeper was collecting it above (him)," Sunil Gavaskar recalled. For many Indians on their first tour to the West Indies, this was quite a change from the usual sight of the wicketkeeper collecting balls around the waist back home[24].

---

24 Sunil Gavaskar at Book Launch of Democracy XI. Sports Tak YouTube Channel: https://www.youtube.com/watch?v=NsndBbv1mBk (At 58:00)

Sardesai was quietly watching along with his teammates. Once he got a good look at the bowling, he proclaimed to his teammates, "He kasle gh***** fast bowler!" (Marathi for: Are they really fast bowlers?) "If these guys are slow, what must Wes (Hall) and Charlie (Griffith) really have been?" Gavaskar thought.

As it turned out, Sardesai walked the talk starting with a brave 212 at Jamaica. That dismissive attitude continued as he amassed 642 runs through the five Tests. In a sense, he was a torchbearer for the Indian team on the tour, particularly for the young Gavaskar, who made an instant impression in his debut series. "Dilip helped bring about a renaissance in Indian cricket. My first Test was in the West Indies in 1971 when Dilip was perhaps at his very best. He showed us how to play fast bowling and in doing so gave us the confidence we needed to beat the West Indies. One of his great strengths was that he was always very positive and he spread that through the team," Gavaskar said in tribute when Sardesai passed away in 2007[25].

25 Sunil Gavaskar's tribute to Dilip Sardesai – ICC Press Release on July 3, 2007. Accessed at: http://archive.indianexpress.com/news/i-looked-up-to-sardesai-gavaskar/203691/1

Dilip Sardesai,
Eknath Solkar and the Ball

At 75 for five in the first innings of the first Test at Jamaica, Eknath Solkar joined Dilip Sardesai in the middle with a mission to resurrect the Indian innings. The two Bombay players then showed remarkable grit to record a 137-run stand. During the partnership, the ball lost its shape and West Indies captain, Garry Sobers, was trying to persuade the umpires to change it. Sardesai and Solkar would join in those discussions, just to balance out Sobers' arguments if and when the decision to change was taken.

Solkar was playing and missing quite a bit during his innings. Once the umpires replaced the ball, he asked Sobers to show it to him. "What's the point? You will play and miss anyway," Sobers remarked. The all-rounder shot back by saying, "You play your game, we will play our game.[26]" It was a typical combative response from a gritty cricketer.

Even after Solkar's fall for 61, Sardesai continued to rally the innings. In Erapalli Prasanna, he found more support during a 122-run stand for the ninth wicket. Sardesai was dismissed for 212 but by then India had a competitive total on the board. They were eventually bowled out for 387.

---

26   Devendra Prabhudesai, SMG – A Biography of Sunil Manohar Gavaskar – Chapter – Bradmanesque Beginning. Published by Rupa and Co 2009

Eknath Solkar brought in a lot of character as a batsman and bowler. However, he was best known for being a great fielder at forward short leg. He took some blinders across India's two tours in 1971.

Kenia Jayantilal's
Only Test Innings

With Sunil Gavaskar still recovering going into the first Test, Kenia Jayantilal was handed a cap at Kingston. When the team to the West Indies was announced, the Hyderabadi opener was one of the youngsters who was earmarked for success. During the 1970-71 season, Jayantilal had scored 473 runs in seven First-Class games to win a spot in the Indian team. Having started the tour with a duck against Jamaica in the first match, he struck form when he hit 58 not out against the West Indies Board President's XI.

At Sabina Park, he walked out to bat with S Abid Ali to take on Vanburn Holder and Grayson Shillingford. Jayantilal made his way to five before Shillingford found his outside edge. The brilliant Garry Sobers dived across to his right to take a great catch as Jayantilal had to make his way back to the pavillion. "I was actually taking my bat away from the ball when it gained a nick and flew to Sobers. He had moved the wrong way when he stopped and came up with a diving catch. Of course, it was a fantastic catch but it spelt doom for me," Jayantilal said[27].

---

27 Vijay Lokapally, Caught but not out, The Hindu – Published on September 25, 2013. Accessed at: https://www.thehindu.com/features/metroplus/caught-but-not out/article5167661.ece

As it turned out, this was his only Test innings, in spite of all the success in the tour games that followed.

India did not bat a second time in the first Test at Kingston with the West Indies being made to follow-on by Ajit Wadekar. In the next Test, Sunil Gavaskar announced his entry into international cricket. While that remained the extent of Jayantilal's Test career, he did make a vital contribution for India during the historic game at The Oval, albeit as a substitute. He took an important catch of Basil D'Oliveira off S Venkataraghavan at a time when India were tightening the noose around England in the second innings.

Sobers Shocked at Imposition of Follow-On at Jamaica

Thanks to a fantastic double century by Dilip Sardesai and his sterling partnerships with Eknath Solkar and Erapalli Prasanna, India posted 387 in the first innings at Sabina Park, Kingston. In reply, the West Indies collapsed to 217 all-out, buckling under the pressure applied by the Indian spinners, Bishan Singh Bedi, Prasanna and S Venkataraghavan. With a lead of 170, India decided to impose the follow-on on Day Four.

Normally, the deficit required to enforce the follow-on is 200. However, since the first day's play was washed out due to rain, this was effectively a four-day game and the deficit required was only 150. Venkataraghavan, the vice-captain, informed Wadekar about this rule. "In those days as a player, I used to take so much interest in reading the rules. I used to know the laws of the game from top to bottom," the off-spinner said[28].

The match was expected to end in a draw and majority of the Indian team was in favour of batting again to get some time in the middle. However, skipper Ajit Wadekar had other ideas and instead put West Indies back in to bat. Not only that, but Wadekar also wanted to play some mind-games – by going to inform the

---

28   Aditya Bhushan and Sachin Bajaj, Fortune Turners: The Quartet that spun India to glory, p. 94. Published by Global Cricket School - 2019

West Indies team before the umpires[29]. "I strutted into the West Indies dressing-room and loudly proclaimed: "Hey Garry, West Indies have to follow on[30]," Wadekar said as the entire West Indies team heard it.

Garry Sobers was shocked as he wasn't aware of the rule in shortened games and double-checked with the umpires. "They were taken aback and that, I think, gave us some psychological edge going forward in the series," Wadekar recalled[31]. India had made the right move and put West Indies under pressure in the first game, having come from behind. Led by Rohan Kanhai's 158 not out, Clive Lloyd's 57 and Garry Sobers's 93, West Indies played out time for a draw after an initial stutter.

29 Ashish Magotra, 'Mr Sobers, would you like to bat?', Rediff. Published on April 18, 2002. Accessed at: https://www.rediff.com/cricket/interview/mr-sobers-would-you-like-to-bat/20180817.htm

30 Ajit Wadekar – as told to H Natarajan – Wisden.com 2002. Accessed at: https://www.espncricinfo.com/story/hey-garry-you-have-to-follow-on-244928

31 When Ajit Wadekar Reminisced The Summer of '71. BCCI Official Website. Published on August 16, 2018. Accessed at: https://www.bcci.tv/articles/2018/news/99893/when-ajit-wadekar-reminisced-the-summer-of-71

West Indies vs India – 1ˢᵗ Test – India tour of West Indies 1971

Dates: 18-23 February 1971 (5-day Test match with rest day on 21 February)
Venue: Sabina Park, Kingston, Jamaica
Toss: West Indies, chose to field
Scores: IND 387 & WI 217, 385/5 (following-on)
Result: Draw
Series status: 0-0

INDIA INNINGS

S Abid Ali	c Camacho b Shillingford	6
K Jayantilal	c Sobers b Shillingford	5
A Wadekar(c)	c Fredericks b Holder	8
D Sardesai	c Findlay b Holder	212
S Durani	b Barrett	13
M Jaisimha	b Holder	3
E Solkar	b Sobers	61
S Venkataraghavan	c Findlay b Sobers	4
P Krishnamurthy†	b Noreiga	10
E Prasanna	b Holder	25
B Bedi	not out	5
Extras	(b 9, lb 6, nb 20)	35
Team score		387

Fall of wickets 1-10, 2-13, 3-36, 4-66, 5-75, 6-212, 7-222, 8-260, 9-382, 10-387

Bowling figures	O	M	R	W
V Holder	27.4	9	60	4
G Shillingford	26	2	70	2
G Sobers	30	8	57	2
J Noreiga	31	7	69	1
A Barrett	35	6	86	1
C Lloyd	4	1	7	0
J Carew	5	2	3	0

WEST INDIES	FIRST INNINGS		SECOND INNINGS	
R Fredericks	c Abid Ali b Prasanna	45	c Krishnamurthy b Bedi	16
S Camacho	c Wadekar b Prasanna	35	c Abid Ali b Venkataraghavan	12
R Kanhai	c sub b Venkataraghavan	56	not out	158
C Lloyd	run out	15	run out	57
G Sobers(c)	c Abid Ali b Prasanna	44	c Krishnamurthy b Solkar	93
J Carew	c Wadekar b Prasanna	3		
A Barrett	c Solkar b Venkataraghavan	2	c Abid Ali b Solkar	4
M Findlay†	b Bedi	6	not out	30
V Holder	b Venkataraghavan	7		
G Shillingford	b Bedi	0		
J Noreiga	not out	0		
Extras	(b 4)	4	(b 9, lb 5, nb 1)	15
Team score		217		385/5

Fall of wickets 1st innings: 1-73, 2-90, 3-119, 4-183, 5-202, 6-203, 7-205, 8-217, 9-217, 10-217

Fall of wickets 2nd innings: 1-18, 2-32, 3-147, 4-320, 5-326

Bowling figures	O	M	R	W	O	M	R	W
S Abid Ali	9	2	30	0	5	2	11	0
E Solkar	2	0	9	0	22	4	56	2
B Bedi	31.5	12	63	2	24	5	63	1
E Prasanna	33	12	65	4	21	5	72	0
S Venkataraghavan	18	5	46	3	37	8	94	1
S Durani	14	0	42	0				
M Jaisimha					13	1	32	0

Dilip Sardesai Ignores Doctor's Instructions

Dilip Sardesai hailed from Goa but travelled to Mumbai as a young man and pursued his cricketing dreams. Along the way, he carried with him a typical Goan's love for food. While he changed India's fortunes in the Caribbean on the field in 1971, he indulged in local delicacies off it and had a great time. However, on one occasion at Trinidad, he fell ill and was advised by the doctor to maintain a liquid diet for three days to recover. Chicken soup was the recommended item in that period.

A few hours later, Sardesai's teammates spotted him feasting on a chicken. "Since chicken soup is made of chicken, why not have the chicken itself," Sardesai told them when they reminded him of the doctor's advice[32].

On the field, Sardesai's appetite for runs was even greater on that tour. Sunil Gavaskar walked away with the major plaudits for his record-breaking 774 runs in his debut series, but it was Sardesai who set the tone and was the torch-bearer for the team. The 642 runs on that tour firmly placed him as the Renaissance Man of Indian cricket and in the process, he had left an indelible mark.

---

32 Close in and personal, Mumbai Mirror. Published on July 4, 2007. Accessed at:https:// mumbaimirror.indiatimes.com/sport/cricket/close-in-personal/articleshow/15721019. cms

In 2007, it was announced that India's best performer in any Test series against West Indies would be honoured with the Dilip Sardesai Award. A fitting tribute to the batsman's legacy!

Andy Roberts Meets the Indians

Following a strong performance in the first Test, India's second stop on the tour was at St Kitts, to take on the Leeward Islands. It was the first time the Indians came face to face with Andy Roberts, then a young fast bowler coming up the ranks in domestic cricket.

When the Indian team landed in St Kitts, an immigration officer warned Dilip Sardesai about the threat ahead. "Now you watch out for this Roberts fella. He gonna knock your head off," he said[33]. However, Sardesai wasn't perturbed as he wasn't going to play the game and instead told the officer to warn Sunil Gavaskar, who was to feature in the match.

Roberts did not have an impact in that game as he went wicketless in both innings. However, Gavaskar scored 82 in the first essay, his maiden First-Class fifty on the tour and then helped India to victory in the second innings with 32 not out.

A few years down the line, Roberts came to India as a finished product and made quite an impression – went on to become one of West Indies' best fast bowlers. In 47 Tests, he finished with 202 wickets – 67 of them coming against India at an average

33 Sunil Gavaskar, Idols, Chapter: Andy Roberts, p.6. Published by Rupa and Co 1983 – Fourth Impression

of 21.70. The St Kitts Immigration Officer was right about the Roberts threat, but was a few years early!

The other future Test players India came across on the tour included the likes of Alvin Kallicharran and Lawrence Rowe to name a few.

Leeward Islands vs Indians – India tour of West Indies 1971 - Tour Match

Dates: 25-28 February 1971 (3-day First-Class match. Rest day on 27 February)
Ground: Warner Park, Basseterre, St Kitts
Toss: Unknown
Scores: IND 361/6d, 60/1 & Leeward Islands 147, 270 (following-on)
Result: Indians won by 9 wickets

INDIANS	FIRST INNINGS		SECOND INNINGS	
A Mankad	b Willett	13	lbw b Willett	13
S Gavaskar	c & b Willett	82	not out	32
K Jayantilal	b Arthurton	21		
M Jaisimha	lbw b Arthurton	3		
S Durani	c Yearwood b Arthurton	37		
A Wadekar(c)	not out	128		
E Solkar	b Williams	1		
S Abid Ali	not out	64	not out	7
Extras	(b 10, lb 2)	12	(b 1, nb 1, w 6)	8
Team Score		361/6d		60/1

Did not bat: D Govindraj, †R Jeejeebhoy, P Krishnamurthy

Fall of wickets 1st innings: 1-47, 2-108, 3-115, 4-124, 5-185, 6-194

Fall of wickets 2nd innings: 1-46

Bowling figures	O	M	R	W	O	M	R	W
A Roberts	14	4	41	0	2	0	10	0
E Arthurton	42	9	93	3	1	0	8	0
L Williams	12	2	38	1	2	0	9	0
E Willett	41	9	123	2	3	0	12	1
J Warrington	23	7	36	0	1	0	13	0
G Yearwood	2	0	11	0				
L Harris	1	0	7	0				

LEEWARD ISLANDS	FIRST INNINGS		SECOND INNINGS	
L Williams	b Jaisimha	29	c Solkar b Jaisimha	41
G Yearwood	c & b Solkar	9	lbw b Solkar	10
L Sergeant	b Solkar	5	c Jeejeebhoy b Durani	56
L Harris(c)	b Jaisimha	18	lbw b Jaisimha	24
A Rouse	lbw b Jaisimha	6	b Jaisimha	1
E Barrett	c Wadekar b Durani	22	c Gavaskar b Jaisimha	10
A Hector†	b Jaisimha	28	c Wadekar b Durani	18
E Arthurton	lbw b Solkar	10	not out	45
E Willett	run out	0	b Durani	2
J Warrington	b Jaisimha	0	b Jaisimha	11
A Roberts	not out	6	b Solkar	27
Extras	(b 4, lb 9, nb 1)	14	(b 9, lb 15, nb 1)	25
Team Score		147		270

Fall of wickets 1st innings: 1-35, 2-43, 3-69, 4-77, 5-82, 6-117, 7-135, 8-136, 9-137, 10-147

Fall of wickets 2nd innings: 1-56, 2-60, 3-61, 4-114, 5-152, 6-164, 7-197, 8-199, 9-216, 10-270

Bowling figures	O	M	R	W	O	M	R	W
D Govindraj	6	1	13	0	5	2	20	0
S Abid Ali	8	5	6	0	4	3	4	0
E Solkar	19	7	43	3	15.3	2	42	2
S Durani	12	4	32	1	30	9	90	3
M Jaisimha	17	7	38	5	37	10	79	5
A Mankad	1	0	1	0				
S Gavaskar	3	0	10	0				

Indian Openers Help Team Recover Sleep

Ahead of the second Test at Port-of-Spain, India were scheduled to play a First-Class encounter against Trinidad and Tobago. However, the scheduling and change in venue stretched Ajit Wadekar and his men, as they only flew into the island in the wee hours of the day. Not only that, but the game was scheduled at the Guaracara Park, Pointe-a-Pierre, which is a good distance away from Port-of-Spain.

The jaded Indian team arrived at the ground for the game and were to bat first. The openers Ashok Mankad and Sunil Gavaskar came to their team's rescue as they occupied the crease and constructed a strong partnership of 155. Mankad was eventually dismissed for 79 as Gavaskar went on to score 125. "We landed at 3am the day we were to play Trinidad and were all sleeping in the dressing room thanks to a long opening stand between Mankad and Gavaskar," Wadekar recalled[34].

The Indians recovered well enough to post 464 in the first innings and warmed up well ahead of the second Test. Although a drawn game, most of their batsmen got the runs and gained confidence going into the Test match.

---

34 Sunder Rajan, India vs West Indies 1971, p. 103. Published by Jaico Publishing House 1971

Eknath Solkar Gets an Interesting Offer

Back in those days, the Caribbean public took great pride in their cricket and loved the game whole-heartedly. The crowds were known to create a festive atmosphere around Test matches with music and chants ringing from the stands. Along the way, they were also known to indulge in friendly banter with the players – at times dishing out some humorous volleys. One such hilarious and notable incident took place during one of the tour matches in 1971.

One of the local batsmen hit a ball high in the air. Eknath Solkar, India's best fielder, was waiting in anticipation to collect the skier when a voice from the stands beamed, "Solkaar! Solkaar! If you drop that catch, you can have my sista [sister]." Unfazed, Solkar did what the team needed and completed a clean catch. As the team huddled up, captain Wadekar asked Solkar if he'd heard the spectator's offer. "Yes, but I've not seen his sister," was Solkar's witty and honest reply[35].

Wadekar also recalled Solkar completing the catch and telling the crowd, "I am already married. Thank you very much![36]"

---

35 When Eknath Solkar got an 'unbelievable offer' to drop a catch, CricketCountry. Published on: June 1, 2015. Accessed at: https://www.cricketcountry.com/criclife/cricketainment/when-eknath-solkar-got-an-unbelievable-offer-to-drop-a-catch-504538

36 Dwarkanath Sanzgiri's YouTube Channel, Eknath Solkar Tribute. Accessed at: https://www.youtube.com/watch?v=c1lOmxo0_SM&t (At 14:50)

'Take Your Time to Bowl Overs'

As was the case in the 1960s, India were heavily dependent on their spinners on the tour to the West Indies in 1971. Eknath Solkar and Abid Ali were the designated medium-pace bowlers while D Govindraj, the only paceman in the side, did not feature in a Test match. In comparison, West Indies had their share of fast bowlers, albeit not as threatening as they were on the previous Indian visit in 1962. Captain Ajit Wadekar realised that India would end up bowling many more overs when compared to their opponents, simply because the spinners take lesser time to complete their deliveries.

Wadekar said, "(Bishan Singh) Bedi normally would bowl his over in around 1.5 minutes and the West Indian fast bowlers would take around six/seven minutes.[37]" West Indies had the likes of Garry Sobers, Clive Lloyd and Rohan Kanhai in their middle-order. Such quality players would only capitalise if they got more balls to face from the Indian spinners. "I told Bedi to take his time and even if he was criticised, I would take the blame," Wadekar said.

Bedi obliged his captain and took his time to complete his overs – although it wasn't as much as the West Indies fast bowlers. It was still enough to implement Wadekar's strategy. As expected, there

---

37   Ashish Magotra, 'Mr Sobers, would you like to bat?', Rediff. Published on April 18, 2002. Accessed at: https://www.rediff.com/cricket/interview/mr-sobers-would-you-like-to-bat/20180817.htm

was criticism from the media but the Indian captain held firm and pointed to the scorecards, which revealed that India bowled more than the hosts.

At every step, Wadekar was a thoughtful leader and his out-of-the-box techniques did their trick across those two tours in 1971.

'Poetry in motion' is what people said when they saw **Bishan Singh Bedi** bowl with his lovely action. He was an integral part of India's triumph in the West Indies and England.

Trinidad and Tobago vs Indians – India tour of West Indies 1971 - Tour Match

Dates: 1-4 March 1971 (4-day First-Class match)
Venue: Guaracara Park, Pointe-a-Pierre, Trinidad
Toss: Indians, chose to bat
Scores: Indians 464/7d & 162/5d, Trinidad & Tobago 338 & 126/0
Result: Draw

INDIANS	FIRST INNINGS		SECOND INNINGS	
A Mankad	lbw b Ali	79	b Julien	1
S Gavaskar	run out	125	c sub b Corneal	63
S Durani	run out	43		
D Sardesai	c Corneal b Ali	92		
G Viswanath	c Gabriel b Julien	1	c Davis b Corneal	16
M Jaisimha	c Bartholomew b Ali	40	not out	25
A Wadekar(c)	not out	41		
E Solkar	b Bartholomew	14		
S Abid Ali	not out	15	not out	10
R Jeejeebhoy†	c Gabriel b Ali	27		
S Venkataraghavan	c Lewis b Ali	12		
Extras	(b 1, lb 6, nb 7)	14	(b 4, nb 3, w 1)	8
Team Score		464/7d		162/5d

Fall of wickets 1st innings: 1-155, 2-240, 3-273, 4-276, 5-387, 6-401, 7-424

Fall of wickets 2nd innings: 1-1, 2-96, 3-98, 4-126, 5-130

Bowling figures	O	M	R	W	O	M	R	W
P Bartholomew	27	5	61	1	5	1	13	0
B Julien	28	7	82	1	5	1	12	1
I Ali	39	5	151	3	24	1	78	2
J Noreiga	44	17	103	0	4	2	3	0
C Davis	20	2	49	0	4	0	20	0
A Corneal					25	13	26	2
B Davis					1	0	2	0

TRINIDAD AND TOBAGO	FIRST INNINGS		SECOND INNINGS	
O Durity	c Viswanath b Jaisimha	80	not out	64
R Gabriel	c sub b Venkataraghavan	26	not out	57
A Lewis†	c Venkataraghavan b Jaisimha	4		
C Davis	c Durani b Wadekar	100		
A Corneal	c Mankad b Abid Ali	17		
B Davis(c)	run out	61		
S Gomes	b Abid Ali	8		
B Julien	lbw b Abid Ali	0		
P Bartholomew	c Wadekar b Venkataraghavan	19		
I Ali	not out	9		
J Noreiga	b Abid Ali	6		
Extras	(b 6, lb 2, nb 4)	8	(b 3, nb 2)	5
Team Score		338		126/0

Fall of wickets 1st innings: 1-62, 2-67, 3-210, 4-230, 5-254, 6-284, 7-284, 8-309, 9-332, 10-338

Bowling figures	O	M	R	W	O	M	R	W
S Abid Ali	24.1	3	80	4	5	2	10	0
E Solkar	6	2	10	0				
S Gavaskar	5	1	11	0	7	0	30	0
S Venkataraghavan	42	10	111	2	1	0	7	0
S Durani	12	3	34	0	8	1	22	0
M Jaisimha	33	16	48	2	3	2	3	0
A Mankad	5	0	22	0	6	1	20	0
A Wadekar	6	1	14	1	3	1	9	0
D Sardesai					10	0	20	0

Abid Ali Takes a Wicket Off the First Ball of the Test Match

S Abid Ali's main role was to help take the shine off the ball before the spinners came into force. However, he could be more than useful with his right-arm medium pace upfront. After all, he started his Test career with a six-for in Australia. When Ajit Wadekar and his men landed in the Caribbean, Abid was the ultimate team-man, having opened the batting as well when needed. However, it was with his bowling that he put his name in the record books. During the second Test at Trinidad, Abid became the first Indian bowler to take a wicket off the first ball of the Test match.

The left-handed Roy Fredericks took strike on what was a tricky-looking surface at the Queen's Park Oval. As Abid got ready to bowl, he heard a voice from the stands saying, "Ali, you can't take a wicket, man, you can't bowl." That man was in for a shock as Fredericks was dismissed bowled off the first ball of the Test match. The West Indian crowds can be very cheeky with their comments but are equally generous. "Ali, you're the greatest," said the same man who had taunted the Hyderabadi all-rounder[38].

---

38 Anindya Dutta, The Greatest Year – The 1971 Tours of West Indies and England, Published By Westland Publications Private Limited 2020

The first ball was an indication of things to come as India went on to bowl the West Indies out for 214 in the first innings. Abid's feat has only been replicated by one other Indian bowler – the great Kapil Dev – who managed to take a wicket off the first ball of a Test match on two occasions.

S Abid Ali became the first Indian bowler to take a wicket off the first ball in a Test match. He also had the distinction of being at the crease when India recorded victories at Trinidad and at The Oval.

Sunil Gavaskar Gets a Reprieve From Garry Sobers

Sunil Gavaskar's century and a fifty in the tour game against Trinidad had assured him of a place in the team for the second Test. The Bombay batsman may have come in with runs and reputation but a few nerves were inevitable as he stepped out into the highest level. India bowled the West Indies out for only 214 following which Gavaskar walked out to bat for the first time in Test cricket. Ashok Mankad, his Bombay colleague, took first strike[39].

Surprisingly, when Gavaskar crossed over to face his first ball, he did not take fresh guard and merely used the one marked out by Mankad[40]. Soon after, he was on his way in Test cricket with his first runs. Early on Day Two, Gavaskar edged one from Vanburn Holder and Garry Sobers, who was known to be a great fielder, dropped one of the simplest of catches in the slips. The Bombay opener made it count with an innings of 65 to begin his Test career with authority. Gavaskar's fortune was in contrast to Kenia Jayantilal, whose only Test innings ended with Sobers taking a blinder at Jamaica. Here, the West Indies captain dropped a catch he would have taken any other day.

---

39   Devendra Prabhudesai, SMG – A Biography of Sunil Manohar Gavaskar – Chapter – Bradmanesque Beginning. Published by Rupa and Co 2009
40   Devendra Prabhudesai, SMG – A Biography of Sunil Manohar Gavaskar – Chapter – Bradmanesque Beginning. Published by Rupa and Co 2009

Gavaskar's run of luck continued even into the next Test at Guyana where Sobers spilled two more chances. He went on to score his first Test century in that match and never looked back!

Back to Trinidad, Dilip Sardesai's 112 guided India to 352 although the West Indies off-spinner Jack Noreiga toiled for nearly 50 overs to bag figures of nine for 95.

Salim Durani's Twin Strikes Turn the Game

The mercurial Salim Durani's Test record doesn't reflect the impact he had on Indian cricket. The enigmatic all-rounder had the ability to stamp his authority on a game-changing moment, helping turn the tide in his team's favour. Back in 1961-62, he played a crucial role in India's home series win against England and then smashed a century batting at No. 3 at Trinidad. Almost nine years down the line, he was one of the senior lieutenants in Ajit Wadekar's team that took on Garry Sobers and his men. At Trinidad in the second Test, Durani delivered the decisive blow that not only turned the game but put India in the driving seat.

When West Indies were bowled out for 214 in the first innings, Erapalli Prasanna and Bishan Singh Bedi led the way for India. Durani's left-arm spin wasn't used. India took a 138-run lead but at the end of Day Three, West Indies were well-placed at 150 for one. That evening, Durani met ML Jaisimha and Prasanna, asking them to convince Wadekar to allow him the opportunity to have a go with the ball.

The next day, India had a bit of luck go their way when Charlie Davis, the unbeaten batsman overnight, was injured in the nets before play and had to be taken to hospital. Roy Fredericks was run out for 80 soon after play resumed. Garry Sobers and Clive Lloyd, West Indies' two key players were at the crease when

Wadekar summoned Durani to work his promised magic. Bowling to Sobers, Durani targeted the rough around the off-stump. "It hit the spot nicely, turned a little, beat his defence, went between bat and pad and took the off stump. He couldn't believe it and walked back muttering, 'Oh, Jesus.' I couldn't control my happiness, and was jumping in jubilation," said Durani[41].

Durani wasn't done there as Lloyd was the other dangerman India wanted to get rid of. Durani and Wadekar had a word and decided that the captain should move to short mid-wicket[42]. "Having made him play a few outside off, I over-pitched one on the off stump, but with a lot of turn," Durani said[43]. Soon enough, Lloyd went for the shot and found Wadekar.

West Indies were now 169 for four and they were eventually bowled out for 261. Davis returned to bat and fought hard during his unbeaten 74 but it wasn't enough. S Venkataraghavan finished with a five-wicket haul. Durani's final analysis read a magnificent 17-8-21-2. India were left with only 124 to get to create history.

41 Nagraj Gollapudi, Dancing in the Lion's Den, The Cricket Monthly, Accessed at: https://www.thecricketmonthly.com/story/326340/dancing-in-the-lion-s-den
42 Anindya Dutta, The Greatest Year – The 1971 Tours of West Indies and England, Published By Westland Publications Private Limited 2020
43 Nagraj Gollapudi, Dancing in the Lion's Den, The Cricket Monthly, Accessed at: https://www.thecricketmonthly.com/story/326340/dancing-in-the-lion-s-den

Wadekar Prays Gavaskar Misses Out on Debut Century

"We, as Indians, are superstitious. It was in my mind that whenever someone scored a century for India on debut, he failed miserably later on," said Ajit Wadekar as Sunil Gavaskar went about constructing a good start in his first Test innings[44]. Wadekar knew of his Bombay colleague's powers of concentration and that once Gavaskar was set, he was capable of making a huge score. Yet, Wadekar the superstitious man trumped Wadekar the captain.

Wadekar said, "I prayed that he does not get a century on his debut, as it is a curse to Indian cricket. Whoever had done that earlier never lasted long in the Indian team.[45]" Up until then, six Indians had scored centuries on Test debut. One of them was in the dressing room that day – Gundappa Viswanath – who had done so during the home series against Australia in 1969. The previous five hadn't scored another century in their respective Test careers. Although one must say Lala Amarnath was one of

---

44   When Ajit Wadekar Reminisced The Summer of '71. BCCI Official Website. Published on August 16, 2018. Accessed at: https://www.bcci.tv/articles/2018/news/99893/when-ajit-wadekar-reminisced-the-summer-of-71

45   Ajit Wadekar, Dravid's men can repeat History, Press Trust of India, Published on: May 14, 2006. Accessed at: https://www.hindustantimes.com/india/dravid-s-men-can-repeat-history/story-iIDF3VXpzdyB2KNMTB7lFO.html

them, who did not make another century, but was an iconic figure in Indian cricket.

Eventually, Viswanath broke the jinx and became the first Indian debut centurion to add another hundred to his tally in Test cricket.

Gavaskar Hits the Winning Runs – India Make History

Once the West Indies were bowled out for 261, India were left with a small matter of 124 to win their first ever Test on Caribbean soil. All eyes were on Sunil Gavaskar and Ashok Mankad when they resumed the run-chase on Day Four. The Bombay batsmen combined well to add 74 before Arthur Barrett struck to dismiss Mankad. Soon after, Salim Durani, batting at No. 3, was bowled. Dilip Sardesai, the centurion from Jamaica and the first innings at Trinidad, was caught behind 10 runs later.

At the other end, Gavaskar maintained his cool. On debut, he had shown remarkable composure and with India on the brink of victory, he was unfazed. Abid Ali was sent in at No. 5 to soak in the pressure and finish the job. In tandem with Gavaskar, they managed to pinch a few quick runs, helping India get closer and closer to the target[46]. As history beckoned, the senior Abid told the debutant, "Go on, you deserve to score the winning runs.[47]"

India's first victory in the Caribbean was achieved when Gavaskar hit one through the leg-side for four. It was not only India's first

---

46   Devendra Prabhudesai, SMG – A Biography of Sunil Manohar Gavaskar – Chapter – Bradmanesque Beginning. Published by Rupa and Co 2009

47   Anindya Dutta, The Greatest Year – The 1971 Tours of West Indies and England, Published By Westland Publications Private Limited 2020

victory in the Caribbean but their maiden one against the West Indies. The closest they had come was back in 1949 where they came within six runs of victory at the Brabourne Stadium, when the umpire infamously declared stumps.

Gavaskar had finished his Test debut with 65 and 67 not out to announce his arrival in Test cricket. At the end of the match, he was awarded the Barclays' Incentive Award – 250 East Caribbean Dollars. Meanwhile, Wadekar picked up a winning cheque of 500 East Caribbean Dollars. Back in those times, these were big amounts for sporting success. It was well-deserved considering how big the occasion was for Indian cricket[48].

---

48 Devendra Prabhudesai, SMG – A Biography of Sunil Manohar Gavaskar – Chapter – Bradmanesque Beginning. Published by Rupa and Co 2009

West Indies vs India – 2nd Test - India tour of West Indies 1971

Dates: 6-10 March 1971 (5-day Test match with rest day on 8 March)
Venue: Queen's Park Oval, Port of Spain, Trinidad
Toss: West Indies, chose to bat
Scores: WI 214, 261 & IND 352, 125/3
Result: India won by 7 wickets
Series Status: India lead the series 1-0

WEST INDIES	FIRST INNINGS		SECOND INNINGS	
R Fredericks	b Abid Ali	0	run out	80
S Camacho	c Solkar b Bedi	18	b Venkataraghavan	3
R Kanhai	c Solkar b Prasanna	37	c Venkataraghavan b Bedi	27
C Lloyd	b Abid Ali	7	c Wadekar b Durani	15
C Davis	not out	71	not out	74
G Sobers(c)	b Venkataraghavan	29	b Durani	0
A Barrett	c Solkar b Prasanna	8	b Venkataraghavan	19
M Findlay†	b Bedi	1	c Solkar b Venkataraghavan	0
V Holder	c Krishnamurthy b Bedi	14	b Venkataraghavan	14
G Shillingford	c Solkar b Prasanna	25	c Durani b Venkataraghavan	1
J Noreiga	b Prasanna	0	c Solkar b Bedi	2
Extras	(b 2, lb 2)	4	(b 18, lb 7, nb 1)	26
Team score		214		261

Fall of wickets 1st innings: 1-0, 2-42, 3-62, 4-62, 5-108, 6-132, 7-133, 8-161, 9-214, 10-214

Fall of wickets 2nd innings: 1-73, 2-150, 3-152, 4-169, 5-169, 6-218, 7-222, 8-254, 9-256, 10-261

Bowling figures	O	M	R	W	O	M	R	W
S Abid Ali	20	4	54	2	5	2	3	0
E Solkar	3	0	12	0	7	2	19	0
S Gavaskar	1	0	9	0				
B Bedi	16	5	46	3	29.5	11	50	2
E Prasanna	19.5	3	54	4	16	5	47	0
S Venkataraghavan	13	0	35	1	36	11	95	5
S Durani					17	8	21	2

INDIA	FIRST INNINGS		SECOND INNINGS	
A Mankad	b Shillingford	44	c sub b Barrett	29
S Gavaskar	c Lloyd b Noreiga	65	not out	67
S Durani	c & b Noreiga	9	b Barrett	0
D Sardesai	c Shillingford b Noreiga	112	c Findlay b Barrett	3
A Wadekar(c)	c Kanhai b Noreiga	0		
E Solkar	c & b Noreiga	55		
S Abid Ali	c Shillingford b Noreiga	20	not out	21
S Venkataraghavan	st Findlay b Noreiga	5		
P Krishnamurthy†	c sub b Noreiga	0		
E Prasanna	not out	10		
B Bedi	c Holder b Noreiga	4		
Extras	(b 18, lb 2, nb 8)	28	(b 2, lb 2, nb 1)	5
Team score		352		125/3

Fall of wickets 1st innings: 1-68, 2-90, 3-186, 4-186, 5-300, 6-330, 7-337, 8-337, 9-342, 10-352

Fall of wickets 2nd innings: 1-74, 2-74, 3-84

Bowling figures	O	M	R	W	O	M	R	W
V Holder	19	8	37	0	2	0	12	0
G Shillingford	20	3	45	1	6	2	13	0
G Sobers	28	7	65	0	15	5	16	0
J Noreiga	49.4	16	95	9	18	4	36	0
A Barrett	37	13	65	0	8.4	0	43	3
C Davis	3	1	11	0				
C Lloyd	1	0	6	0				

S Venkataraghavan was appointed deputy to Ajit Wadekar in 1971.
He delivered with a crucial five-wicket haul during India's win at
Trinidad. In the decisive fifth Test, he contributed with an important
fifty.

Dilip Sardesai Pranks
Salim Durani

When India beat West Indies in the second Test at Trinidad, the enormity of the occasion dawned on everyone involved. That India had managed to beat West Indies for the first time in their history, that too in their backyard, was truly special. More so, Trinidad is known to have a huge Indian diaspora and while the victory may have been miles away from home, the conditions and the atmosphere made the tourists feel comfortable. With all this in the backdrop, Dilip Sardesai decided to prank his roommate Salim Durani.

Durani was in their room when he answered the telephone. "Mr Durani, we are happy you won us the game. We are Indians staying here. We would like to meet you at the reception," someone said in a West Indian accent. The friendly Durani rushed downstairs to meet and greet his fans, but didn't find anyone. He went back to his room, when the same person called and said they were by the swimming pool, adding a big promise to that. "We want to present you with a camera and TV," the voice beamed. Durani went by the pool this time and yet again, there was no one[49].

49   Makarand Waingankar, Dilip Sardesai: The Renaissance Man of Indian Cricket, Times of India. Published on March 22, 2012. Accessed at: https://timesofindia. indiatimes.com/sports/new-zealand-in-india-2016/top-stories/Dilip-Sardesai-The-renaissance-man-of-Indian-cricket/articleshow/12363876.cms

Watching all this from a corner, Sardesai finally approached his roommate. Durani eventually connected the dots and realised he was being pranked!

Rohan Kanhai Comes to Kenia Jayantilal's Rescue

One of Kenia Jayantilal's greatest worries ahead of India's tour to the West Indies was food. For an Indian vegetarian, travelling to other countries can be challenging and the opener was making his first trip to the Caribbean. In Rohan Kanhai, Jayantilal found a saviour. The West Indian great assured him that vegetarian food wouldn't be a problem.

"In Guyana, I got a lot of vegetarian food like bhindi masala, puran poli, biryani, baingan ka shaag. Everyday there was some change," Jayantilal recalled[50]. Most of the groundsmen and those who worked on the grounds were of Indian origin and they helped out Jayantilal on Kanhai's suggestion. "Rohan knew everybody and he told me 'Don't worry. You will get vegetarian food'," he said.

Jayantilal continued to get vegetarian food through the trip. Some of his teammates then told him, "Thoda zyada mangao. Hum non-veg kha kha ke bore ho gaye." (Hindi for: Order some more. We are bored of eating non-veg)

Kanhai was known to be friendly with the opposition and was particularly encouraging of youngsters. This was yet another example of his gregarious nature.

---

50 Conversation with the author

Rohan Kanhai was one of West Indies' finest batsmen. A genial man,
Kanhai was respected by the opposition. On India's visit to the West
Indies in 1971, he ensured that the vegetarian Kenia Jayantilal did
not struggle for options. He also encouraged a young Sunil Gavaskar
during his first series.

Jayantilal Scores Century but Misses Out on Test Selection

Sunil Gavaskar had announced himself to Test cricket with impressive half-centuries in each innings at Trinidad. While Ashok Mankad had done a decent job at the other end, Kenia Jayantilal fancied his chances of making it back into the team when he was brought in for the tour game against Guyana. He scored 59 in the first innings and then an unbeaten 122 in the second essay. Jayantilal had pushed his case to walk out alongside Gavaskar at Bourda, Georgetown.

Rohan Kanhai, the West Indies batsman, believed Jayantilal had a good chance of playing the third Test. "In the evening he (Kanhai) told me, 'I think you will be playing the next Test match'," Jayantilal recalled[51]. However, when the Test match started three days later, Jayantilal found his name was missing from the playing XI.

He said, "On the day of the match, the team was announced and I was 12th man. Kanhai came personally and said, 'Bad luck, boy!'" In terms of averages on tour, Jayantilal finished only behind Gavaskar and Dilip Sardesai. He finished with 506 First-Class runs in seven matches at an average of 56.22 with one century and four fifties.

---

51 Conversation with the author

At Guyana, India brought in Gundappa Viswanath into the side to play his first Test of the tour. ML Jaisimha, who also got a century in the tour game against Guyana, missed out as well. Mankad, who scored a fifty in the second innings of the tour game against Guyana, was retained as an opener. In the Test match, Gavaskar scored his first international century at Guyana and Mankad too managed a few runs. The door shut for Jayantilal on the Caribbean trip.

Kenia Jayantilal had a great time in First-Class matches in the West Indies. However, his Test career was limited to the solitary appearance in Jamaica. Sunil Gavaskar came into the side in the second Test and the rest is history.

Guyana vs Indians – India tour of West Indies 1971 - Tour Match

Dates: 13-16 March 1971 (4-day First-Class match)
Toss: Guyana, chose to bat
Venue: Bourda, Georgetown
Scores: Guyana 382 & 206/6d, Indians 262 & 277/3
Result: Draw

GUYANA	FIRST INNINGS		SECOND INNINGS	
R Fredericks	c Bedi b Venkataraghavan	95	lbw b Govindraj	0
M Pydanna†	c Viswanath b Durani	32	not out	1
C Lloyd	c Jeejeebhoy b Durani	57	c & b Bedi	17
A Kallicharran	b Venkataraghavan	8	c Viswanath b Durani	55
R Ramnarace	c & b Bedi	4	run out	4
B Butcher	c Jeejeebhoy b Abid Ali	36	c Jayantilal b Venkataraghavan	44
R Kanhai(c)	b Venkataraghavan	92	run out	34
L Cornelius	c Jeejeebhoy b Govindraj	8	not out	42
K Glasgow	c Viswanath b Venkataraghavan	13		
S Shivnarine	b Durani	9		
L Gibbs	not out	11		
Extras	(b 4, lb 8, nb 5)	17	(b 4, lb 4, nb 1)	9
Team Score		382		206/6d

Fall of wickets 1st innings: 1-91, 2-187, 3-191, 4-196, 5-204, 6-301, 7-319, 8-355, 9-362, 10-382

Fall of wickets 2nd innings: 1-0, 2-91, 3-107, 4-108, 5-150, 6-203

Bowling figures	O	M	R	W	O	M	R	W
D Govindraj	11	1	67	1	5	2	25	1
S Abid Ali	13	2	34	1	3	0	18	0
B Bedi	34	5	99	1	12	1	54	1
S Venkataraghavan	29	9	69	4	15	6	47	1
S Durani	17.5	1	63	3	14	2	45	1
M Jaisimha	12	3	33	0	1	0	8	0

INDIANS	FIRST INNINGS		SECOND INNINGS	
A Mankad	c Pydanna b Ramnarace	0	c Ramnarace b Gibbs	52
K Jayantilal	c & b Glasgow	59	not out	122
S Durani	b Cornelius	15	st Pydanna b Cornelius	24
G Viswanath	lbw b Glasgow	25	c & b Shivnarine	44
M Jaisimha	c & b Shivnarine	108		
S Abid Ali	lbw b Cornelius	14	not out	25
S Venkataraghavan(c)	c Kanhai b Glasgow	18		
P Krishnamurthy	b Shivnarine	3		
D Govindraj	lbw b Shivnarine	3		
B Bedi	b Shivnarine	0		
R Jeejeebhoy†	not out	0		
Extras	(b 11, lb 6)	17	(lb 7, nb 1, w 2)	10
Team Score		262		277/3

Fall of wickets 1st innings: 1-0, 2-31, 3-70, 4-186, 5-212, 6-253, 7-253, 8-259, 9-259, 10-262

Fall of wickets 2nd innings: 1-121, 2-158, 3-232

Bowling figures	O	M	R	W	O	M	R	W
R Ramnarace	21	6	48	1	19	3	42	0
K Glasgow	25	7	45	3	22	2	53	0
L Gibbs	30	13	41	0	18	4	39	1
L Cornelius	21	5	55	2	14	2	38	1
S Shivnarine	21.5	8	29	4	27	6	60	1
B Butcher	4	0	7	0				
R Kanhai	1	1	0	0	2	1	2	0
C Lloyd	5	0	19	0	3	0	13	0
R Fredericks	1	0	1	0				
A Kallicharran					3	0	20	0

Sardesai Asks Sobers to Walk Off

Going into the second innings of the third Test at Guyana, West Indies captain Garry Sobers felt the pressure to perform. Post his 93 in the second innings at Jamaica, Sobers had made scores of 29, zero and four. On Day Five at Guyana, a draw seemed the most likely result but Sobers wanted to make a statement. Early in his innings, he was tested by the Indian spinners and the tourists believed they had him on one occasion.

Dilip Sardesai was standing close-in when Salim Durani came on to bowl with Sobers still in single-figures. Sobers tried to play forward to Durani but the ball lobbed off the pad and was pouched by Sardesai. The Indians appealed in unison, convinced that they had a good shout. The umpire turned it down! Durani couldn't believe it and appealed a second time. The umpire was firm! The dejected Durani then threw the ball to the ground to express his disgust[52].

A good sportsman that Sobers was, he may have walked off in any other situation. However, the circumstances were different considering his personal run of form and his team's situation in the series. Sardesai, who wasn't the best of fielders, then quipped to Sobers, "Garry, that was my first ever catch. Why don't you just walk off?"

---

52 West Indies vs India, 3rd Test match Report – November 30, 1971, Wisden. Accessed at: https://www.espncricinfo.com/story/west-indies-v-india-150254

Sobers replied, "I didn't hear what you said." The entire Indian team on the field was in splits[53].

The West Indies captain went on to get 108 not out and declared with the Test match meandering towards a draw. During this century, he also reached 7,000 Test runs. The Indian openers batted out 30 overs to complete the formalities.

53   Close in and personal, Mumbai Mirror. Published on July 4, 2007. Accessed at: https://mumbaimirror.indiatimes.com/sport/cricket/close-in-personal/articleshow/15721019.cms

West Indies vs India – 3rd Test - India tour of West Indies 1971

Dates: 19-24 March 1971 (5-day Test match with rest day on 22 March)
Venue: Bourda, Georgetown, Guyana
Toss: WI, chose to bat
Scores: WI 363, 307/3d, IND 376 & 123/0
Result: Draw
Series status: India lead the series 1-0

WEST INDIES	FIRST INNINGS		SECOND INNINGS	
R Fredericks	c Abid Ali b Venkataraghavan	47	lbw b Solkar	5
J Carew	c Mankad b Durani	41	c Durani b Bedi	45
R Kanhai	c Krishnamurthy b Bedi	25		
C Lloyd	run out	60	c Krishnamurthy b Bedi	9
C Davis	lbw b Solkar	34	not out	125
G Sobers(c)	c Venkataraghavan b Bedi	4	not out	108
D Lewis†	not out	81		
K Boyce	c Gavaskar b Venkataraghavan	9		
G Shillingford	c Bedi b Venkataraghavan	5		
L Gibbs	run out	25		
J Noreiga	run out	9		
Extras	(b 11, lb 9, nb 3)	23	(b 5, lb 6, nb 4)	15
Team Score		363		307/ 3d

Fall of wickets 1st innings: 1-78, 2-119, 3-135, 4-213, 5-226, 6-231, 7-246, 8-256, 9-340, 10-363

Fall of wickets 2nd innings: 1-11, 2-114, 3-137

Bowling figures	O	M	R	W	O	M	R	W
S Abid Ali	13.2	5	42	0	14	2	55	0
E Solkar	17	3	34	1	16	4	43	1
S Venkataraghavan	59	14	128	3	20	10	47	0
B Bedi	55	18	85	2	26	9	55	2
S Durani	14	3	51	1	16	2	47	0
A Mankad					5	0	33	0
A Wadekar					3	0	12	0

INDIA	FIRST INNINGS		SECOND INNINGS	
A Mankad	b Noreiga	40	not out	53
S Gavaskar	c Carew b Sobers	116	not out	64
A Wadekar(c)	b Sobers	16		
G Viswanath	b Boyce	50		
S Durani	lbw b Sobers	2		
D Sardesai	run out	45		
E Solkar	run out	16		
S Abid Ali	not out	50		
S Venkataraghavan	lbw b Shillingford	12		
P Krishnamurthy†	run out	0		
B Bedi	lbw b Boyce	2		
Extras	(b 5, lb 6, nb 15, w 1)	27	(b 4, nb 1, w 1)	6
Team score		376		123/0

Fall of wickets 1st innings: 1-72, 2-116, 3-228, 4-244, 5-246, 6-278, 7-339, 8-370, 9-374, 10-376

Bowling figures	O	M	R	W	O	M	R	W
K Boyce	20.4	5	47	2	2	0	12	0
G Shillingford	21	2	76	1	2	0	13	0
G Sobers	43	15	72	3	5	1	14	0
L Gibbs	39	17	61	0	1	0	4	0
J Noreiga	42	9	91	1	10	0	30	0
J Carew	2	0	2	0				
C Lloyd					3	0	20	0
R Fredericks					4	0	9	0
C Davis					3	0	15	0

Govindraj Catches the Eye at Barbados

D Govindraj, the Hyderabad player, was the only proper fast bowler in the Indian team across the two tours in 1971. However, he was unfortunate to not get a Test match and only featured in the tour matches. India were heavily reliant on their spinners and the likes of Abid Ali and Eknath Solkar's medium pace would help ready the ball before they came on. However, during India's tour game against Barbados ahead of the fourth Test, Govindraj had an interesting duel with Garry Sobers.

Spurred on by his Hyderabad teammate, ML Jaisimha, Govindraj bowled a bouncer to Sobers. The West Indian great let that delivery go through to the wicketkeeper. Jaisimha asked Govindraj for an encore, which brought out a belligerent reply from Sobers. "The next moment I see Sobers hitting a flat six over Jaisimha's head, who was fielding at mid-off. Sobers had a big grin as he saw Jai giving instructions to me," Govindraj said[54].

The duel did not end there. Sobers, who scored 135 in that innings, was eventually bowled by Govindraj. "I had tears in my eyes," Govindraj said years later.

---

54 N Jagannath Das, Govindraj, meet the country's fastest bowler of the 60s, Telangana Today, Published on May 8, 2020. Accessed at: ,https://telanganatoday. com/govindraj-meet-the-countrys-fastest-bowler-of-60s

It was during that game that Govindraj met Charlie Griffith, the former West Indies fast bowler, who had felled Nari Contractor during India's previous visit in 1962. "You bowling bouncers to Garry maan with these shoulders?" Griffith exclaimed as he held Govindraj by his shoulders[55]. Govindraj also won praise for his bowling action from Clyde Walcott[56].

Interestingly, Govindraj got married to a Guyanese girl that year. He was out of the India reckoning after the England tour and gave up the game in 1974.

---

55 Arunabha Sengupta, D Govindraj, Member of the history making '71 team reveals little-known facts. Accessed at: https://www.cricketcountry.com/articles/d-govindraj-member-of-the-history-making-71-indian-team-reveals-little-known-facts-18207

56 N Jagannath Das, From a batsman to a fast bowler, Telangana Today. Published on May 26, 2019. Accessed at: https://telanganatoday.com/from-a-batsman-to-a-fast-bowler

D Govindraj was India's only quick bowler on both tours in 1971 but did not play a Test match.

Barbados vs Indians – India tour of West Indies 1971 - Tour Match

Dates: 27-30 March 1971 (4-day First-Class match)
Venue: Kensington Oval, Bridgetown, Barbados
Toss: Barbados, chose to field
Scores: Indians 185 & 313, Barbados 449 & 52/1
Result: Barbados won by 9 wickets

INDIANS	FIRST INNINGS		SECOND INNINGS	
S Gavaskar	run out	0	b Holder	67
K Jayantilal	lbw b Boyce	40	lbw b Sobers	76
A Wadekar(c)	b Shepherd	42	c Nurse b Howard	67
G Viswanath	b Shepherd	10	c Nurse b Holder	24
S Durani	c Howard b Shepherd	1	b Howard	33
M Jaisimha	c Nurse b Shepherd	12	run out	5
E Solkar	c Nurse b Holder	22	not out	14
S Abid Ali	c Boxill b Hall	41	lbw b Sobers	0
D Govindraj	b Holder	0	c Holder b Sobers	4
R Jeejeebhoy†	not out	5	b Howard	3
E Prasanna	c Boxill b Hall	1	b Howard	6
Extras	(lb 7, nb 4)	11	(b 2, lb 2, nb 10)	14
Team Score		185		313

Fall of wickets 1st innings: 1-2, 2-60, 3-84, 4-86, 5-114, 6-114, 7-166, 8-172, 9-179, 10-185

Fall of wickets 2nd innings: 1-149, 2-151, 3-203, 4-272, 5-283, 6-293, 7-294, 8-301, 9-306, 10-313

Bowling figures	O	M	R	W	O	M	R	W
W Hall	8	1	25	2	10	0	36	0
V Holder	15	3	41	2	17	6	33	2
K Boyce	8	1	37	1	15	2	32	0
J Shepherd	14	3	40	4	12	2	28	0
G Sobers	6	1	23	0	22	8	29	3
D Holford	2	0	8	0	23	6	78	0
A Howard					24.4	5	59	4
M Bynoe					2	1	4	0

BARBADOS	FIRST INNINGS		SECOND INNINGS	
M Bynoe	c Solkar b Abid Ali	48	not out	25
P Lashley	c Wadekar b Abid Ali	8	b Govindraj	0
S Nurse	c Jeejeebhoy b Abid Ali	0	not out	26
G Sobers(c)	b Govindraj	135		
D Holford	b Solkar	111		
J Shepherd	c Jayantilal b Govindraj	2		
K Boyce	run out	74		
D Boxill†	b Abid Ali	29		
W Hall	b Abid Ali	10		
A Howard	run out	16		
V Holder	not out	5		
Extras	(b 1, lb 5, nb 5)	11	(lb 1)	1
Team Score		449		52/1

Fall of wickets 1st innings: 1-50, 2-52, 3-75, 4-288, 5-290, 6-364, 7-395, 8-419, 9-438, 10-449

Fall of wickets 2nd innings: 1-13

Bowling figures	O	M	R	W	O	M	R	W
D Govindraj	20	1	101	2	4	0	32	1
S Abid Ali	32.5	7	107	5				
E Prasanna	22	2	99	0				
S Durani	9	0	30	0				
M Jaisimha	13	1	26	0	2	0	6	0
E Solkar	16	1	75	1	2.2	0	13	0

Ajit Wadekar Wins First Toss as Test Captain on Birthday

In his first three Tests as captain of India, Ajit Wadekar didn't have the best luck with the coin. The rub of the green went against him in each of those matches as Garry Sobers won those tosses. However, the fourth Test started on April 1, 1971, which was Wadekar's 30th birthday. This time, the coin favoured the birthday boy as the Indian captain put the West Indies in to bat. Most people were surprised by the decision to bowl first.

Ahead of the Test match, the Barbados Cricket Association presented the Indian captain with a cake. India though had a tough day in the field as West Indies piled the runs after being put in to bat, ending Day One on 224 for three. "The atmosphere in Barbados was cloudy and heavy and the West Indies had four pace bowlers. I think Garry would have put us in had he won the toss," Wadekar explained later[57]. The brains trust of the Indian team – Wadekar, Dilip Sardesai and ML Jaisimha – were all in agreement that West Indies should be put in to bat. In the tour game before the match, Barbados had beaten India by nine wickets. India were shot out for 185 while batting first on Day One.

---

57 Sunder Rajan, India vs West Indies 1971, p. 100. Published by Jaico Publishing House 1971

At the end of Day Two, West Indies had piled 501 for five and Sunil Gavaskar's early dismissal in fading light had left India at two for one. "I tell you, you should have seen our faces that evening," said Wadekar[58].

Thereafter, India had to battle to save the game – which they eventually did thanks to a fighting century by Sardesai in the first innings. Gavaskar then delivered with another century in the second essay to take India to safety.

---

58   Ajit Wadekar, My Most Awkward Moments As Captain, The Illustrated Weekly of India, Vol C, June 10-16, 1979, p. 29-30

Sardesai Tricks Sobers Into Keeping the Spinner On

Captain Ajit Wadekar's decision to put West Indies in to bat at Barbados in the fourth Test backfired as Garry Sobers's 178 not out powered the hosts to 501 for five. In reply, slumped to 70 for six, leaving Dilip Sardesai and Eknath Solkar with the task of rescuing India again. The duo bettered their effort from the first Test in Jamaica adding 186 in tandem. Solkar was eventually dismissed for 65 but Sardesai went on to get 150 and help India avoid the follow-on.

During the Sardesai-Solkar stand, the former came up with an ingenious solution to keep the fast bowlers away and make Sobers persist with Inshan Ali, the spinner, who wasn't threatening the Indian batsmen. West Indies had fast bowlers such as Vanburn Holder, John Shepherd and debutant Uton Dowe, who could have possibly troubled the tourists more than the spinners.

"Let's pretend we can't read his (Ali) googly, let's play and miss to see if Sobers will keep him on," Sardesai told Solkar[59]. Sobers fell for the ruse and kept Ali into the attack, which in turn helped the Indian batsmen tick the score along. West Indies lost the opportunity to possibly press the issue.

---

59   Dilip Sardesai, How We Broke Through In '71, The Illustrated Weekly of India, Vol C, June 10-16, 1979, p. 33

While Sobers was arguably the greatest cricketer in that era, he wasn't known for his captaincy. "In fact, if Sobers is a good captain, I'm the best fielder in the world," Sardesai remarked in his typical humorous style[60].

---

60 Ibid

The 'Rennaisance Man' **Dilip Sardesai** inspired India with some great
performances on the tour to the West Indies. He amassed 642 runs
during the five-match Test series.

Sunil Gavaskar vs Uton Dowe

While West Indies did not have famed fast bowlers during the Indian visit in 1971, a youngster by the name of Uton Dowe was seen as one for the future. The Jamaican could bowl fast and had already faced-up to the Indians earlier on the tour during the first game. The Indian captain Ajit Wadekar had copped one on the hand in that opening encounter but had bravely soldiered on to set an example for the team. By the time the fourth Test commenced in Barbados and the hosts were trailing 0-1, they decided to field Dowe in an attempt to add bite to the bowling attack.

Sunil Gavaskar, fresh from his maiden Test century at Guyana, took on Dowe to commence the Indian innings in the face of a mammoth 501 by the hosts. It was the evening of Day Two with the sun setting on the shores. Gavaskar appealed to the umpires about the light but his requests were turned down. Dowe, fired up on debut, gave the young opener a customary fast bowler's stare. Uncharacteristically, Gavaskar tried to hook a short one from Dowe but found the man at mid-wicket. India were two for one! Interestingly, play was soon called off due to bad light[61].

The incident made Gavaskar introspect and he famously wrote a letter back home, promising and assuring his loved ones that,

---

61 Devendra Prabhudesai, SMG – A Biography of Sunil Manohar Gavaskar – Chapter – Bradmanesque Beginning. Published by Rupa and Co 2009

"I have learnt a lesson. Henceforth, I will only show my back to the bowler.[62]"

Gavaskar more than lived up his promise with three centuries in the remaining three Test innings on the tour. In the second essay at Barbados, Gavaskar's unbeaten 117 helped India avoid defeat in the face of a 335-run target. India finished on 221 for five – comfortably drawing the game.

---

62 Sunder Rajan, India vs West Indies 1971, p. 100. Published by Jaico Publishing House 1971

West Indies vs India – 4th Test - India Tour of West Indies 1971

Dates: 1-6 April 1971 (5-day Test match with rest day on 5 April)
Venue: Kensington Oval, Bridgetown, Barbados
Toss: India, chose to field
Scores: WI 501/5d, 180/6d & IND 347, 221/5
Result: Draw
Series status: India lead the series 1-0

WEST INDIES	FIRST INNINGS		SECOND INNINGS	
R Fredericks	b Abid Ali	1	b Venkataraghavan	48
D Lewis†	b Bedi	88	c Abid Ali	14
R Kanhai	c Mankad b Venkataraghavan	85	c Krishnamurthy b Solkar	11
C Davis	c Venkataraghavan b Abid Ali	79	not out	22
G Sobers(c)	not out	178	c Bedi b Abid Ali	9
C Lloyd	c Mankad b Bedi	19	c Venkataraghavan b Abid Ali	43
M Foster	not out	36	not out	24
J Shepherd	c Solkar b Venkataraghavan	3		
Extras	(b 10, lb 4, nb 1)	15	(b 2, lb 3, nb 1)	6
Team score		501/5d		180/6d

Did not bat – I Ali, V Holder, U Dowe

Fall of wickets 1st innings: 1-4, 2-170, 3-179, 4-346, 5-394

Fall of wickets 2nd innings: 1-17, 2-36, 3-112, 4-126, 5-132, 6-133

Bowling figures	O	M	R	W	O	M	R	W
S Abid Ali	31	1	127	2	21	3	70	3
E Solkar	19	4	40	0	14	0	73	1
M Jaisimha	10	2	32	0				
B Bedi	54	15	124	2	1	0	6	0
S Venkataraghavan	57	12	163	1	7	0	25	2

INDIA	FIRST INNINGS		SECOND INNINGS	
A Mankad	c Lewis b Holder	6	c Shepherd b Ali	8
S Gavaskar	c Holder b Dowe	1	not out	117
P Krishnamurthy†	c Ali b Dowe	1		
A Wadekar(c)	c Lewis b Sobers	28	c Lloyd b Sobers	17
G Viswanath	c Lewis b Sobers	25	c Shepherd b Sobers	0
D Sardesai	lbw b Holder	150	c Fredericks b Shepherd	24
M Jaisimha	b Dowe	0	lbw b Dowe	17
E Solkar	c Lewis b Dowe	65	not out	10
S Abid Ali	run out	9		
S Venkataraghavan	b Shepherd	12		
B Bedi	not out	20		
Extras	(b 6, lb 6, nb 18)	30	(b 2, lb 8, nb 17, w 1)	28
Team score		347		221/5

Fall of wickets 1st innings: 1-2, 2-5, 3-20, 4-64, 5-69, 6-70, 7-256, 8-269, 9-285, 10-347

Fall of wickets 2nd innings: 1-35, 2-71, 3-79, 4-132, 5-192

Bowling figures	O	M	R	W	O	M	R	W
V Holder	25.4	7	70	2	8	4	13	0
U Dowe	23	7	69	4	11	5	22	1
J Shepherd	24	4	54	1	20	7	36	1
G Sobers	20	9	34	2	23	8	31	2
I Ali	20	4	60	0	18	1	65	1
M Foster	11	3	28	0	14	7	10	0
C Davis	2	0	2	0	3	2	1	0
C Lloyd					4	0	13	0
R Fredericks					1	0	1	0
R Kanhai					1	0	1	0

Mountain Chicken in Dominica and the Delayed Game

The West Indies are a diverse set of islands, with different cultures, political systems etc. but only unite to play cricket. A tour across the Caribbean would give one a peek into the diversity in every aspect. The Indian team got a taste of that during their hectic tour to the Caribbean in 1971 which took them across six nations. One of their tour games was against the Windward Islands on the island nation of Dominica. In doing so, India also became the first visiting team to play a match in the island of Dominica and were greeted with a lot of fanfare upon arrival[63].

During that visit, the Indians were recommended a local delicacy called "Mountain Chicken". The foodies in the team had no hesitation in calling for a portion and had a feast enjoying the succulent meat. "The gourmets in our team wolfed down whole portions of it, for it was soft, sweet and tender," captain Ajit Wadekar observed[64]. Little did they know that in local parlance, "Mountain Chicken" actually referred to a preparation of wild frogs. Of course, it left the foodies shell-shocked when they found out what it really was.

---

63   Sunder Rajan, India vs West Indies 1971, p. 81. Published by Jaico Publishing House 1971

64   My Cricketing Years, Ajit Wadekar as told to KN Prabhu, p. 29. Published by Vikas Publishing House Pvt Ltd 1973

The visit to Dominica was for India's last First-Class encounter ahead of the fifth and final Test at Trinidad. Windward Islands and India played out a draw. Incidentally, this match was postponed because India's flight from Barbados was delayed by a day. Thus one of the rest days, i.e. April 9, was canned and play was scheduled, although it was Good Friday[65].

65   Cricket Archive Scorecard

Windward Islands vs Indians – India tour of West Indies 1971 - Tour Match

Dates: 8-10 April 1971 (3-day First-Class match)
Venue: Botanical Gardens, Roseau, Dominica
Toss: Indians, chose to field
Scores: Windward Islands 207 & 171/9d, Indians 197/9d & 92/2
Result: Draw

WINDWARD ISLANDS	FIRST INNINGS		SECOND INNINGS	
V Elwin	st Jeejeebhoy b Venkataraghavan	19	b Govindraj	10
G Alfred	b Bedi	20	c Jaisimha b Govindraj	5
I Shillingford(c)	lbw b Venkataraghavan	6	c Jeejeebhoy b Venkataraghavan	32
H Williams	b Durani	3	c Jeejeebhoy b Venkataraghavan	4
R Polius	c & b Bedi	21	c Govindraj b Venkataraghavan	1
V Bute	c Gavaskar b Bedi	13	c Viswanath b Bedi	23
M Findlay†	c Jeejeebhoy b Solkar	62	c Viswanath b Bedi	21
G Shillingford	b Bedi	3	c Govindraj b Jaisimha	12
N Phillip	lbw b Durani	16	b Govindraj	38
M Francis	c Jeejeebhoy b Govindraj	28	not out	6
G Gibbs	not out	1		
Extras	(b 12, lb 2, nb 1)	15	(b 7, lb 10, nb 2)	19
Team Score		207		171/ 9d

Fall of wickets 1st innings: 1-35, 2-39, 3-48, 4-48, 5-83, 6-98, 7-102, 8-140, 9-205, 10-207

Fall of wickets 2nd innings: 1-20, 2-27, 3-35, 4-37, 5-70, 6-92, 7-120, 8-140, 9-171

Bowling figures	O	M	R	W	O	M	R	W
D Govindraj	11	5	17	1	8.5	2	17	3
E Solkar	10	4	11	1	1	0	3	0
M Jaisimha	8	3	25	0	8	2	23	1
B Bedi	33	14	52	4	21	10	44	2
S Venkataraghavan	27	7	59	2	21	9	54	3
S Durani	13	5	28	2	4	1	9	0
S Gavaskar					1	0	2	0

INDIANS	FIRST INNINGS		SECOND INNINGS	
S Gavaskar	c Findlay b Phillip	14	b G Shillingford	12
K Jayantilal	c Findlay b G Shillingford	65		
A Wadekar(c)	c Findlay b Gibbs	41		
G Viswanath	c I Shillingford b Francis	12	not out	16
S Durani	c I Shillingford b Francis	11	not out	34
M Jaisimha	run out	0		
E Solkar	c Alfred b Francis	5		
S Venkataraghavan	c Phillip b Francis	15		
R Jeejeebhoy†	c Findlay b Gibbs	5	c Williams b Gibbs	29
D Govindraj	not out	23		
Extras	(b 2, lb 2, nb 2)	6	(nb 1)	1
Team Score		197/ 9d		92/ 2

Did not bat: B Bedi

Fall of wickets 1st innings: 1-17, 2-80, 3-95, 4-115, 5-115, 6-122, 7-148, 8-157, 9-197

Fall of wickets 2nd innings: 1-12, 2-49

Bowling figures	O	M	R	W	O	M	R	W
G Shillingford	11.5	1	45	1	5	0	34	1
N Phillip	17	6	26	1	6	4	12	0
M Francis	29	5	78	4	7	3	9	0
G Gibbs	24	10	42	2	5	0	26	1
H Williams					1	0	1	0
V Bute					1	1	0	0
V Elwin					1	0	1	0
G Alfred					1	0	1	0
I Shillingford					1	0	7	0

Sobers and Wadekar Feel They Have Won the Toss

The stage was set at the Queen's Park Oval, Trinidad for the fifth and final Test! The visitors were back on the ground they had made history a few weeks ago. The hosts were under pressure having been kept at bay by the tourists! Pride was at stake for the West Indies, who hadn't won a Test series since their tour to India in 1966-67. During their previous home series in 1968, England had walked away with the Wisden Trophy.

Garry Sobers walked out for the toss, with an eye on a win – which wouldn't have given them the series but saved them from conceding the rubber. In such an atmosphere, Sobers's act at the toss in the fifth Test reflected great sportsmanship and revealed why he was respected not only as a cricketer but as an icon. Back in Guyana, Sobers didn't walk when the Indians believed he was caught close-in. At Trinidad, Sobers showed true sportsmanship.

The coin went up for the toss and both captains felt they had won it. "There was a gentleman by the name of Ken Laughlin who went close to the square and faced the crowd and hit his chest to indicate West Indies had won the toss," Joseph Perreira, the West Indian commentator recalled[66].

---

66 The man who could do everything, The Cricket Monthly, Published: July 2016. Accessed at: https://www.thecricketmonthly.com/story/1027587/players--writers-and-commentators-share-their-favourite-garry-sobers-stories

Sobers turned to Wadekar to say that he will inform him of his choice soon. "No, Garry, I won the toss. I'll tell you," was Wadekar's reply. However, Sobers let Wadekar decide and conceded that India had won the toss. As a result, India elected to bat in the all-important game. It was obvious this time that the team winning the toss would want to bat first and bat long, in order to consolidate their position in the Test match.

Led by Sunil Gavaskar's 124, Dilip Sardesai's 75 and S Venkataraghavan's 51, India put up 360 in the first innings. As we know, the match finished in a draw and gave India the series win.

Sobers' Superstition and Wadekar's Response

Going into the last day of the fifth Test at Trinidad, India were in control of proceedings and could entertain thoughts of creating history by sealing a draw. However, Ajit Wadekar was wary of his opposite number, Garry Sobers, whose talismanic and game-changing abilities were no secret. Following a relatively slow start to the series, the southpaw had hit centuries in three consecutive Test matches, which included one in the first innings of the fifth Test. If he got going on the last day, he could deny India their much-wanted shot at history.

Through the series, Sobers had this practice of greeting all the Indian players in the dressing room before day's play. The West Indian legend would then tap Gavaskar on the shoulder as he believed it brought him good luck – with those three centuries being evidence to back the ritual. However, on that day at the Queen's Park Oval, Wadekar wasn't planning on allowing Sobers the opportunity to complete his feel-good superstition.

As Sobers approached the Indian dressing room, the captain pushed Gavaskar into the washroom and locked the door. Sobers went around as usual but could not find Gavaskar and left without tapping him. When Wadekar let Gavaskar out, the latter wasn't amused and told his captain that the West Indian great could very well touch him out in the middle. Wadekar responded by saying, "He only gets runs when he touches you in the dressing room![67]"

As luck would have it, Sobers was bowled first ball by Abid Ali during West Indies' frantic pursuit of 262. Wadekar looked at Gavaskar with a look of vindication! West Indies' innings closed at 165 for eight, drawing the Test which handed India the series 1-0.

67 Ajit Wadekar's superstition about Sunil Gavaskar and Garry Sobers worked, CricketCountry. Published on June 8, 2015. Accessed at: https://www. cricketcountry.com/criclife/cricketainment/ajit-wadekars-superstition-about-sunil-gavaskar-and-garry-sobers-worked-504743

Garry Sobers led from the front with three centuries in the Test series but could not prevent a West Indian defeat.

Sunil Gavaskar Battles Toothache to Join Doug Walters in Elite Club

Sunil Gavaskar's epic effort in the fifth Test at Trinidad is a part of Indian cricket folklore. At the age of 21, the opener showed maturity way beyond his years, coupled with immaculate powers of concentration. In the first innings, he scored 124 to help setup a total of 360. West Indies then took a crucial 166-run lead to put pressure on the Indians. Since this was a deciding Test of the series, it was designated as a six-day affair. India had to keep West Indies at bay with a little over two days to go. In walked Gavaskar and he spent nearly nine hours at the crease for an epic 220. In the process, Gavaskar became the second man in Test history to score a century and a double hundred in one match – emulating the Australian Doug Walters, who recorded the feat against West Indies in 1969.

The second highest score after Gavaskar's 220 in the second innings was captain Ajit Wadekar's 54 – his first fifty of the Test series. Gundappa Viswanath (38) and ML Jaisimha (23) spent crucial time in the middle. This was to be Jaisimha's last Test innings, but he had done his job for the team in this innings. For Gavaskar, it was special as Jaisimha was someone he looked up to and the man was at the other end when he completed his first double century in Test cricket. Through the tour, Jaisimha had prepared for the fast bowlers' challenge by having the reserve wicketkeeper Rusi Jeejeebhoy give him short throwdowns with a wet tennis-ball[68].

These efforts helped India bat into the sixth day and left West Indies with little time to get the target.

While the world praised Gavaskar for his marathon effort, the youngster was battling enormous tooth pain during the Test match. During a net session ahead of the game, a thirsty Gavaskar downed some water from a pitcher. However, a small piece of ice lodged into a cavity in his teeth – causing him immense pain. Such was the pain that his sleep patterns took a hit. To make matters worse, the manager Keki Tarapore forbade him from getting an extraction or relying on medicines to soothe the pain during the Test for the risk of side-effects. Thus, a very weary Gavaskar featured in the all-important game. It was only after he was dismissed on the final day and with India in a position of strength that the manager permitted Gavaskar to get the tooth extracted[69]. The numbers and the scoreboard reflect the magnitude of Gavaskar's effort but the backdrop puts it into true perspective. It was not only a 'Test' of his batsmanship but also his character.

68 Wadekar's Warriors Event. Accessed at: https://youtu.be/ATVNi2CFEfE (At 2:45:35)

69 Sunil Gavaskar, Sunny Days – Sunil Gavaskar's Own Story p 51-58, Published by Rupa and Co. Nineteenth Impression 2005

"It was Gavaskar... De real master," sang Lord Relator in the famous
Calypso. A total of 774 runs in his debut Test series.
Need we say more...

Wadekar Lifted on Shoulders at Queen's Park Oval

The pressure was on West Indies on the last day of the fifth Test at Trinidad. The paucity of time meant that West Indies had to have a go at the 262-run target. Clive Lloyd led the way with an attacking 64 but the target was too steep and West Indies eventually ended the day on 165 for eight. The six-day drawn affair meant that India walked home with the 'rubber' owing to their win in the second Test. While the players understood the importance of the occasion, the Indian-origin people of Trinidad too soaked in the moment at the Queen's Park Oval.

The crowd stormed onto the field and lifted Wadekar on their shoulders. "They bore me shoulder-high from the field and massed in front of our pavillion to cheer all our players," Wadekar said[70].

"As the game ended, hundreds of Trinidadians of east Indian descent, who had strongly supported their kith and kin through the two Tests at Queen's Park, streamed across the ground and lifted Ajit Wadekar on their shoulders. But the biggest cheers were for Gavaskar," said famous West Indies cricket commentator Tony Cozier[71].

---

70 My Cricketing Years, Ajit Wadekar as told to KN Prabhu, p. 87. Published by Vikas Publishing House Pvt Ltd 1973
71 Wisden Asia Cricket, December 2004, Vol 4, No. 1 p.67

Earlier in the day, Gavaskar had completed his marathon effort of 220, while battling a nagging toothache. The Indians had become the talk of the town. Keki Tarapore, the manager, couldn't contain his emotion and is said to have shed a tear or two. From being dubbed a "club side" on arrival at Jamaica in February 1971, they had shattered all those notions from the naysayers.

West Indies vs India – 5th Test - India Tour of West Indies 1971

Dates: 13-19 April 1971 (6-day Test match with rest day on 16 April)
Venue: Queen's Park Oval, Port of Spain, Trinidad
Toss: India, chose to bat
Scores: IND 360, 427 & WI 526, 165/8
Result: Draw
Series result: India won the Test series 1-0

INDIA	FIRST INNINGS		SECOND INNINGS	
S Abid Ali	c Davis b Sobers	10	lbw b Sobers	3
S Gavaskar	c Lewis b Holford	124	b Shepherd	220
A Wadekar(c)	c Sobers b Shepherd	28	c Shepherd b Noreiga	54
D Sardesai	c Lewis b Holford	75	c & b Foster	21
G Viswanath	c Lewis b Shepherd	22	b Sobers	38
M Jaisimha	c Carew b Dowe	0	lbw b Shepherd	23
E Solkar	c sub b Dowe	3	c Sobers b Noreiga	14
S Venkataraghavan	c Carew b Shepherd	51	b Noreiga	21
P Krishnamurthy†	c Lewis b Noreiga	20	c sub b Noreiga	2
E Prasanna	c Lloyd b Holford	16	not out	10
B Bedi	not out	1	c Sobers b Noreiga	5
Extras	(lb 1, nb 9)	10	(b 6, lb 8, nb 2)	16
Team score		360		427

Fall of wickets 1st innings: 1-26, 2-68, 3-190, 4-238, 5-239, 6-247, 7-296, 8-335, 9-354, 10-360

Fall of wickets 2nd innings: 1-11, 2-159, 3-194, 4-293, 5-374, 6-377, 7-409, 8-412, 9-413, 10-427

Bowling figures	O	M	R	W	O	M	R	W
G Sobers	13	3	30	1	42	14	82	2
U Dowe	29	1	99	2	22	2	55	0
J Shepherd	35	7	78	3	24	8	45	2
C Davis	10	0	28	0	10	2	12	0
J Noreiga	16	3	43	1	53.4	8	129	5
D Holford	28.3	5	68	3	27	3	63	0
M Foster	2	0	4	0	12	4	10	1
J Carew					7	2	15	0

WEST INDIES	FIRST INNINGS		SECOND INNINGS	
J Carew	c Wadekar b Prasanna	28	run out	4
D Lewis†	c Krishnamurthy b Bedi	72	not out	4
R Kanhai	run out	13	b Abid Ali	21
C Davis	c Solkar b Venkataraghavan	105	c Viswanath b Venkataraghavan	19
C Lloyd	c Venkataraghavan b Prasanna	6	c Wadekar b Venkataraghavan	64
G Sobers(c)	b Prasanna	132	b Abid Ali	0
M Foster	b Abid Ali	99	run out	18
D Holford	st Krishnamurthy b Venkataraghavan	44	c Bedi b Solkar	9
J Shepherd	c Abid Ali b Venkataraghavan	0	c & b Abid Ali	9
U Dowe	lbw b Venkataraghavan	3	not out	0
J Noreiga	not out	0		
Extras	(b 14, lb 8, nb 2)	24	(b 9, lb 8)	17
Team score		526		165/ 8

Fall of wickets 1st innings: 1-52, 2-94, 3-142, 4-153, 5-330, 6-424, 7-517, 8-522, 9-523, 10-526

Fall of wickets 2nd innings: 1-10, 2-16, 3-50, 4-50, 5-101, 6-114, 7-152, 8-161

Bowling figures	O	M	R	W	O	M	R	W
S Abid Ali	31	7	58	1	15	1	73	3
E Solkar	11	1	35	0	13	1	40	1
B Bedi	71	19	163	1	2	1	1	0
E Prasanna	65	15	146	3	5	0	23	0
S Venkataraghavan	37.3	6	100	4	5	1	11	2
M Jaisimha	1	1	0	0				

From Lord Relator's Calypso to Gavasinder Singh

Once Sunil Gavaskar finished the West Indies tour with a staggering 774 runs, the accolades from all corners were natural – from trophies, awards to cash prizes. However, there were two tributes that stood out for they were touching and sweet.

Bishan Singh Bedi, the Indian left-arm spinner, became a father during the fifth Test at Trinidad. He then announced that he was naming his new-born 'Gavasinder' – in tribute to Gavaskar's achievements in the Caribbean. "To name him Gavasinder Singh, I thought that was fantastic. That's one of the nicest things that has happened," Gavaskar said years later on a talk show[72].

The other tribute came from Lord Relator, a Trinidadian calypso artist, who penned a musical tribute to Gavaskar while watching him bat on that tour in 1971. The song sets the stage by describing a "lovely day for cricket" and goes on to mention several Indian players before elaborating on the West Indian woes. The heart of the song calls Gavaskar as the "real master", beautifully painting his genius musically...

"It was Gavaskar
De real master

---

72 Breakfast with Champions, Sunny's greatest cricketing memories! Accessed at: https://youtu.be/rzh0sHUM_yI (At 16:18)

Just like a wall
We couldn't out Gavaskar at all,
not at all
You know the West Indies couldn't out Gavaskar at all"

"In Trinidad, there's a thing called Badge on. Badge on is like a hooligan who isn't afraid of anybody. And when Sunil played here, he showed he wasn't afraid of anybody. Fans loved him so much because he wasn't afraid of anybody. That is why I wrote about him," Lord Relator said[73]. That fearless attitude exhibited in his maiden series was only a precursor of the many more great performances that were to come in the years ahead.

It wasn't until 1974 that Gavaskar found out about the Calypso, thanks to Andy Roberts who gave him the recording when India toured England that year. Roberts was playing for Hampshire then[74].

73 Somshuvra Laha, Lord Relator: When Sunny Was On Song, Hindustan Times. Published on August 21, 2016. Accessed at: https://www.hindustantimes.com/sports-newspaper/lord-relator-when-sunny-was-on-song/story-FicIqgwGqIOeKPByQkQEgN.html

74 Breakfast with Champions, Sunny's greatest cricketing memories! Accessed at: https://youtu.be/rzh0sHUM_yI (At 15:43)

Triumphant Return from the West Indies

The success in the West Indies caused a sense of euphoria back home in India. It was evident when Ajit Wadekar and his men arrived in Bombay in the wee hours of an April morning in 1971. Thousands of fans had thronged to the airport to meet and greet their heroes, despite the early hours. There were banners reading "Golden Age of Indian Cricket – Sobers Sobered" and "Welcome Home Heroes" to mention a few[75].

The celebrations started as the team deboarded with Sunil Gavaskar proudly displaying the trophy presented to him by Trinidad's cricketing body. Once the team cleared customs, Ajit Wadekar and the young Gavaskar were the cynosure of all eyes, standing on a table high above the others – waving to the crowd that had come to greet them. The players were quite moved by the whole display of appreciation. The Central Government sent the Minister of Education, Siddhartha Shankar Ray, to Bombay to welcome the team at the airport. Maharashtra's Minister for Food and Civil Supplies, HG Vartak, was also present to extend his wishes on behalf of the state.

---

75 India West Indies 1971, Glimpse of Port of Spain, Gavaskar felicitations, Wadekar introduces team, Jai Galagali's YouTube Channel - https://youtu.be/Il0nAqifu-c (At 08:38)

The Bombay Cricket Association (BCA) then held a special ceremony at the Brabourne Stadium to felicitate the whole team. However, it was Gavaskar who was the toast of the nation as numerous awards came his way in the days after the return from the West Indies. Amidst euphoria, the selectors, Wadekar and the players had their eyes on the England tour, where their skills would be tested again.

The celebrations were fitting but bigger things were in store for Wadekar and his men.

India Tour of West Indies 1971 – Tour Statistics

By Kaustubh Gudipati

First-Class batting and fielding record of Indians

Player	M	I	R	NO	AVG	H	F	HS	C	S
S Gavaskar	8	16	1,169	4	97.41	5	6	220	3	0
D Sardesai	8	13	883	0	67.92	3	3	212	0	0
K Jayantilal	7	11	506	2	56.22	1	4	122*	3	0
A Wadekar	11	16	625	2	44.64	1	4	128*	11	0
S Abid Ali	10	17	355	8	39.44	0	2	64*	9	0
E Solkar	10	14	337	2	28.08	0	4	65	12	0
S Durani	10	16	402	1	26.80	1	0	131	5	0
A Mankad	8	16	389	1	25.93	0	3	79	4	0
G Viswanath	7	13	283	1	23.58	0	1	50	7	0
S Venkataraghavan	10	12	233	1	21.18	0	1	51	7	0
M Jaisimha	10	16	312	1	20.80	1	0	108	2	0
R Jeejeebhoy	6	7	69	2	13.80	0	0	29	11	1
E Prasanna	5	7	68	2	13.60	0	0	25	0	0
D Govindraj	5	5	43	1	10.75	0	0	23*	3	0
B Bedi	9	9	37	4	7.40	0	0	20*	8	0
P Krishnamurthy	8	9	56	0	6.22	0	0	20	7	1

First-Class bowling record of Indians

Player	O	M	W	AVG	FW	TW	BBI
S Venkataraghavan	508.1	133	41	31.17	1	0	5/95
M Jaisimha	178	50	13	32.38	2	1	5/38
B Bedi	507.2	154	33	34.39	1	0	5/94
A Wadekar	12	2	1	35.00	0	0	1/14
S Abid Ali	269.2	54	22	37.50	1	0	5/107
D Govindraj	91.5	15	10	37.60	0	0	3/17
S Durani	195.5	41	13	42.07	0	0	3/63
E Prasanna	205.5	52	13	43.23	0	0	4/54
E Solkar	205.5	37	13	46.23	0	0	3/43
S Gavaskar	17	1	0	-	-	-	-
A Mankad	23	2	0	-	-	-	-
D Sardesai	10	0	0	-	-	-	-

Test batting record for India

Player	M	I	R	NO	AVG	H	F	HS
S Gavaskar	4	8	774	3	154.80	4	3	220
D Sardesai	5	8	642	0	80.25	3	1	212
E Solkar	5	7	224	1	37.33	0	3	65
A Mankad	3	6	180	1	36.00	0	1	53*
E Prasanna	3	4	61	2	30.50	0	0	25
G Viswanath	3	5	135	0	27.00	0	1	50
S Abid Ali	5	7	119	2	23.80	0	1	50*
A Wadekar	5	7	151	0	21.57	0	1	54
S Venkataraghavan	5	6	105	0	17.50	0	1	51
B Bedi	5	6	37	3	12.33	0	0	20*
M Jaisimha	3	5	43	0	8.60	0	0	23
S Durani	3	4	24	0	6.00	0	0	13
P Krishnamurthy	5	6	33	0	5.50	0	0	20
K Jayantilal	1	1	5	0	5.00	0	0	5

Test bowling record for India

Player	M	I	O	M	W	AVG	FW	BBI
S Venkataraghavan	5	10	289.3	67	22	33.81	1	5/95
E Prasanna	3	6	159.5	40	11	37.00	0	4/54
B Bedi	5	10	310.4	95	15	43.73	0	3/46
S Abid Ali	5	10	164.2	29	11	47.54	0	3/70
S Durani	3	4	61.0	13	3	53.66	0	2/21
E Solkar	5	10	124.0	19	6	60.16	0	2/56
S Gavaskar	4	1	1.0	0	0	-	-	-
A Wadekar	5	1	3.0	0	0	-	-	-
A Mankad	3	1	5.0	0	0	-	-	-
M Jaisimha	3	3	24.0	4	0	-	-	-

Test batting record for West Indies

Player	M	I	R	NO	AVG	H	F	HS
C Davis	4	8	529	4	132.25	2	3	125*
M Foster	2	4	177	2	88.50	0	1	99
D Lewis	3	5	259	2	86.33	0	3	88
G Sobers	5	10	597	2	74.62	3	1	178*
R Kanhai	5	9	433	1	54.12	1	2	158*
R Fredericks	4	8	242	0	30.25	0	1	80
C Lloyd	5	10	295	0	29.50	0	3	64
D Holford	1	2	53	0	26.50	0	0	44
L Gibbs	1	1	25	0	25.00	0	0	25
J Carew	3	5	121	0	24.20	0	0	45
S Camacho	2	4	68	0	17.00	0	0	35
M Findlay	2	4	37	1	12.33	0	0	30*
V Holder	3	3	35	0	11.66	0	0	14
K Boyce	1	1	9	0	9.00	0	0	9
A Barrett	2	4	33	0	8.25	0	0	19
G Shillingford	3	4	31	0	7.75	0	0	25
J Shepherd	2	3	12	0	4.00	0	0	9
J Noreiga	4	5	11	2	3.66	0	0	9
U Dowe	2	2	3	1	3.00	0	0	3
I Ali	1	-	-	-	-	-	-	-

Test bowling record for West Indies

Player	M	I	O	M	W	AVG	FW	BBI
J Noreiga	4	7	220.2	47	17	29.00	2	9/95
K Boyce	1	2	22.4	5	2	29.50	0	2/47
J Shepherd	2	4	103.0	26	7	30.42	0	3/78
V Holder	3	5	82.2	28	6	32.00	0	4/60
G Sobers	5	9	219.0	70	12	33.41	0	3/72
U Dowe	2	4	85.0	15	7	35.00	0	4/69
D Holford	1	2	55.3	8	3	43.66	0	3/68
A Barrett	2	3	80.4	19	4	48.50	0	3/43
M Foster	2	4	39.0	14	1	52.00	0	1/10
G Shillingford	3	5	75.0	9	4	54.25	0	2/70
I Ali	1	2	38.0	5	1	125.00	0	1/65
R Kanhai	5	1	1.0	0	0	-	-	-
R Fredericks	4	2	5.0	0	0	-	-	-
J Carew	3	3	14.0	4	0	-	-	-
C Lloyd	5	4	12.0	1	0	-	-	-
L Gibbs	1	2	40.0	17	0	-	-	-
C Davis	4	6	31.0	5	0	-	-	-

Key: M – Matches, I – Innings, R – Runs, Avg – Average, HS – Highest Score, H – Hundreds, F – Fifties, NO – Not Outs, O – Overs, W – Wickets, FW – Five Wickets, TW – Ten Wickets, BBI – Innings Best Bowling.

The Sunil Gavaskar Fund and Vijay Merchant's Response

When Everton Weekes made waves during West Indies' tour to India in 1948-49, the *Times of India* had setup a fund to honour him, whereby readers could contribute money to it. The proceeds of the fund were to go to the player directly. Come April 1971, Sunil Gavaskar's record-breaking feats in the Caribbean persuaded the newspaper to do the same and they started off by pooling in Rs 1,001. They then asked interested readers to chip in with a minimum of Rs. 5 contributions[76].

Vijay Merchant, the chairman of selectors, wasn't very impressed with *Times of India's* gesture and believed that such a contribution should benefit the whole team instead of an individual player. Writing to the newspaper, Merchant suggested that such a gesture may imply that a player like Dilip Sardesai's feats in the Caribbean are being ignored. After all, Sardesai too had a big role to play in India's successful campaign in the West Indies.

When Merchant was asked about the repercussions of players accepting such a fund at a time when they were technically

76 Devendra Prabhudesai, SMG – A Biography of Sunil Manohar Gavaskar – Chapter – Bradmanesque Beginning. Published by Rupa and Co 2009

amateurs, he said, "If Sunil Gavaskar does accept the proceeds of a fund without concerning his amateur status, why not the members of the team?[77]"

---

77 Khalid A-H Ansari – Interview with Merchant, Sportsweek, May 2, 1971, p. 32

BCCI Negotiates for a Longer England Visit to India

As the Indian team returned home from their successful tour to the West Indies, the Board of Control for Cricket in India (BCCI) were in discussions with the Marylebone Cricket Club (MCC) about England's reciprocal visit in 1971.

The BCCI wanted England to play three matches against assorted sides along with five zonal games and the five Tests. However, the MCC only agreed to the five Tests and five zonal matches. They also refused to play a festival match, which was intended to be a benefit game for some of India's retired cricketers. The MCC believed it would be a huge workout for the players post a busy summer at home with Tests against both Pakistan and India. Thereafter, they were to host Australia in 1972 for the Ashes.

For years, the tours to the sub-continent hadn't been taken very seriously by the Englishmen as they generally sent in second-string sides on previous visits. "Will the same experiments be continued? The answer will depend on how we fare on the coming tour of England, beginning in June," a report in *Sportsweek* noted in May 1971[78].

Eventually, the MCC visited only in 1972-73 and played the five Tests, five zonal games and one match against the Board

---

78   MCC prefer truncated tour of India, Sportsweek, May 2, 1971, p. 2

President's XI. However, despite India's Test series win in England in 1971, the MCC did not send their full-strength side. That the captain Tony Lewis made his Test debut during the tour to India reflects that fact. The Indian tour was a part of a sub-continental sojourn which also took them to Ceylon (as Sri Lanka was known then) and Pakistan.

Engineer, Chandra Recalled

Farokh Engineer, who had been India's premier wicketkeeper through the late 1960s, missed out on the tour to the West Indies due to the Board's policy of selecting only those who featured in India's domestic season. While P Krishnamurthy 'kept in all five Tests in the Caribbean and Rusi Jeejeebhoy served as a backup, there was a lot of talk about the possibility of Engineer returning to the side for the England tour. After all, he had spent a good amount of time in the country, plying his trade for the county Lancashire. It made cricketing sense to bring back Engineer.

When Vijay Merchant was asked about the Board's policy at the end of the West Indies tour, he said, "I would like to offer no comments on a policy decision made unanimously by the Board.[79]" However, the Board softened its stance and Engineer was selected for the England tour, but due to his commitments to Lancashire, he was only allowed to play the Test matches. Although, he did manage to play a solitary tour game against Glamorgan. Syed Kirmani, the young wicketkeeper, was also picked in the side along with Krishnamurthy. Jeejeebhoy was dropped.

Bhagwat Chandrasekhar was recalled to the Indian Test side with Salim Durani making way. Apart from the twin-strikes at Trinidad, the enigmatic all-rounder hadn't made much of an impact on the series. ML Jaisimha was also axed and never played

---

79   Khalid A-H Ansari – Interview with Merchant, Sportsweek, May 2, 1971, p. 29

Test cricket again. His Hyderabadi teammate Abbas Ali Baig, who had famously made a century on Test debut during the 1959 tour to England, was recalled.

Jaisimha had made many invaluable tactical contributions on the tour to the West Indies but hadn't made enough runs. "I felt sad to see him dropped, but then he just hadn't the runs to recommend his case for England," Ajit Wadekar said[80].

---

80   Ajit Wadekar, My Most Awkward Moments As Captain, The Illustrated Weekly of India, Vol C, June 10-16, 1979, p. 29

The enigmatic **Salim Durani** scored a century against Jamaica in the first game of the tour but did not have much of an impact with the bat later. With the ball, he struck with crucial wickets of Sir Garry Sobers and Sir Clive Lloyd at Trinidad to help put India on the path to victory. However, Durani was dropped for the England tour.

Col Hemu Adhikari Takes Over from Keki Tarapore

In the middle of May 1971, the Indian selectors were to meet to pick the team for the tour to England. The manager Keki Tarapore had submitted his report from the West Indies tour and there weren't any major issues to talk about. The success in the West Indies meant that there weren't any questions over Ajit Wadekar's captaincy despite the fact that he hadn't contributed a lot with the bat. Wadekar was very much the man to captain the Indians on the upcoming tour to England. However, there was a change in personnel as Col Hemu Adhikari took over from Tarapore as manager. Also, Ram Prakash Mehra joined in on the tour as an official to help out Adhikari.

Tarapore and Adhikari were like chalk and cheese. On the one hand, Tarapore was a one-Test wonder, Adhikari had played 21 matches and had also captained India in one game. Interestingly, Adhikari's lone Test century came in Tarapore's solitary appearance for India, which was against West Indies at Delhi in 1948-49.

While Tarapore was more easy-going, Adhikari had his regimen set like an army man. Tarapore also did not interfere in tactical matters, Adhikari was keen to contribute. Through the tour to England, the former India captain contributed with his inputs, which proved crucial at times. "He was not only manager of the team but also its coach," Wadekar remarked[81].

Prior to departure to England, Adhikari instituted more fitness drills and training regimes for the team[82]. Once they were in England, he kept a close eye on all players, being a stickler for discipline.

81 My Cricketing Years, Ajit Wadekar as told to KN Prabhu, p. 14-17. Published by Vikas Publishing House Pvt Ltd 1973

82 Sunil Gavaskar, Sunny Days – Sunil Gavaskar's Own Story p 59, Published by Rupa and Co. Nineteenth Impression 2005

Vijay Merchant Tells Chandrasekhar to Perform

Bhagwat Chandrasekhar had picked up an injury on the tour to Australia in 1967-68 and was then sent back home. Soon after, he was also injured in a road accident. Although picked for the 1969-70 home series against Australia, the leg-spinner did not make it to the playing XI in any of the Test matches. Vijay Merchant, the chairman of selectors, was known to be a purist and it is believed Chandrasekhar's unorthodox way of playing cricket didn't appeal to the man who mattered. As a result, the leg-spinner wasn't picked for the tour to the West Indies.

However, Chandrasekhar's international career was handed a lease of life when he was selected for the tour to England. This came at the back of a good campaign in the Ranji Trophy. Merchant though wasn't very upbeat about Chandrasekhar's selection. He made no secret of the fact that he felt it was a gamble. When the team met Merchant ahead of its flight to England, the chairman of selectors told the leggie, "Chandrasekhar, we are taking a calculated risk with you. It is up to you to prove yourself.[83]"

The mild-mannered leg-spinner was stunned. Having not played a Test for over three years, borne the brunt of an injury and a road accident, the odds were stacked against him. What happened next

---

83 Rajan Bala, The Winning Hand, Biography of BS Chandrasekhar. Published by Rupa and Co 1993, p. 85

is a part of Indian cricketing folklore! Chandrasekhar may have been through all those tough times, but his character helped him deliver when it mattered most and created history in England.

"I am sure the man changed his opinion after the England tour in 1971. Not that I ever cared to find out," Chandrasekhar later said[84]. His performance had done the talking!

---

84 Ibid

Astrologer's Advice Pushes Board to Change Departure Date to England

Cricketers can be a superstitious lot. Some have set rituals such as wearing the left pad first or entering the arena with the right leg first up. A few even carried 'lucky' items such as a handkerchief to the crease. However, rarely would you find an official administration adhere to such routines or rituals. The success in the West Indies pushed the Board of Control for Cricket in India (BCCI) to walk the superstitious line and heed to the advice of an astrologer.

A Dr Thakore, who was a practicing doctor in Mumbai, dabbled in astrology alongside his profession. Ahead of the tour to the Caribbean, it was Dr Thakore who had foreseen India's series win. Thus, when he suggested that the team should depart for England on June 17, 1971, the advice was duly noted and the tickets were booked accordingly[85]. Originally, India were scheduled to travel to England two days earlier.

The tour was to begin on June 23 with a match against Middlesex at Lord's. The Indian team had about five days to acclimatise to the conditions and gear up for the gruelling cricketing season ahead in Old Blighty.

---

85 My Cricketing Years, Ajit Wadekar as told to KN Prabhu, p. 14-17. Published by Vikas Publishing House Pvt Ltd 1973

High Commissioner Accurately Predicts India's Victory

India began their campaign in England with a strong performance against Middlesex in their tour opener at Lord's. Although Middlesex had taken a significant first innings lead, India had the hosts at 99 for seven in the second innings at the end of Day Two, and the tourists believed that any target could be achieved the following day. That same evening, the Marylebone Cricket Club (MCC) hosted a party for the visitors and one of the invitees was the Indian High Commissioner to the United Kingdom – Appa Saheb Pant.

In a chat with Ajit Wadekar during the party, Pant presented his wish-list for the Test series, saying that he hoped for one draw, one rain-affected Test and finally a victory for India to end the series at The Oval. "In the end, it turned out exactly as he had wished," said Wadekar[86].

While India had done wonders by winning in the West Indies, England was still a challenge, considering the fact that they were a strong side. They had come off an Ashes victory in Australia and were a formidable force at home. The team had the belief, but most would have been cautiously optimistic. For Pant to get it exactly right was amazing!

---

86 My Cricketing Years, Ajit Wadekar as told to KN Prabhu, p. 91-92. Published by Vikas Publishing House Pvt Ltd 1973

Middlesex vs Indians – India tour of England 1971 - Tour Match

Dates: 23-25 June 1971 (3-day First-Class match)
Venue: Lord's, London
Toss: Unknown
Scores: Middlesex 233 & 131, Indians 168 & 198/8
Result: Indians won by 2 wickets

MIDDLESEX	FIRST INNINGS		SECOND INNINGS	
E Russell	c Abid Ali b Bedi	84	c Wadekar b Bedi	13
M Smith	c Abid Ali b Bedi	54	b Venkataraghavan	16
P Parfitt	st K'murthy b Venkataraghavan	18	c Venkataraghavan b Bedi	14
N Featherstone	c V'raghavan b Chandrasekhar	33	c Wadekar b Venkataraghavan	0
C Radley	c Solkar b Bedi	9	c Gavaskar b Bedi	8
M Brearley(c)	c K'murthy b Chandrasekhar	7	b Venkataraghavan	0
J Murray†	c & b Chandrasekhar	6	st Krishnamurthy b Venkataraghavan	26
K Jones	not out	10	c Krishnamurthy b Bedi	6
H Latchman	lbw b Venkataraghavan	2	c Wadekar b Bedi	23
S Black	c K'murthy b Chandrasekhar	0	b Bedi	18
J Price	c K'murthy b Chandrasekhar	2	not out	0
Extras	(b 3, lb 4, nb 1)	8	(b 3, lb 1, nb 3)	7
Team score		233		131

Fall of wickets 1st innings: 1-89, 2-154, 3-164, 4-186, 5-201, 6-217, 7-218, 8-221, 9-229, 10-233

Fall of wickets 2nd innings: 1-24, 2-28, 3-32, 4-32, 5-44, 6-76, 7-83, 8-103, 9-122, 10-131

Bowling figures	O	M	R	W	O	M	R	W
S Abid Ali	7	1	31	0	7	3	10	0
E Solkar	4	0	23	0	5	1	9	0
S Gavaskar	2	0	3	0				
B Bedi	32	12	53	3	26.2	12	29	6
B Chandrasekhar	27.5	5	67	5	14	1	35	0
S Venkataraghavan	21	4	48	2	17	5	41	4

INDIANS	FIRST INNINGS		SECOND INNINGS	
S Gavaskar	c & b Latchman	25	c sub b Price	19
A Ali Baig	c Featherstone b Price	7	c Murray b Black	4
A Wadekar(c)	c Jones b Price	0	run out	33
D Sardesai	c Smith b Latchman	16	c Murray b Price	0
S Venkataraghavan	c Parfitt b Latchman	4	b Parfitt	22
G Viswanath	run out	60	c Smith b Jones	5
E Solkar	c & b Jones	8	c Brearley b Jones	41
S Abid Ali	b Parfitt	29	c Brearley b Featherstone	61
P Krishnamurthy†	b Price	2	not out	1
B Bedi	not out	5	not out	4
B Chandrasekhar	b Price	0		
Extras	(b 4, lb 6, nb 2)	12	(b 5, lb 1, nb 2)	8
Team score		168		198/ 8

Fall of wickets 1st innings: 1-22, 2-22, 3-40, 4-46, 5-67, 6-94, 7-160, 8-161, 9-168, 10-168

Fall of wickets 2nd innings: 1-4, 2-34, 3-34, 4-39, 5-79, 6-135, 7-192, 8-193

Bowling figures	O	M	R	W	O	M	R	W
J Price	17.5	7	31	4	13	3	43	2
K Jones	16	6	30	1	14	2	43	2
H Latchman	23	7	53	3	14	5	37	0
S Black	5	1	16	0	6	0	16	1
P Parfitt	11	3	26	1	21	8	45	1
N Featherstone					4	3	6	1

Essex vs Indians – India tour of England 1971 - Tour Match

Dates: 26-29 June 1971 (3-day Test match with rest day on 27 June)
Venue: Garrison 'A' Cricket Ground, Colchester
Toss: Indians, chose to bat
Scores: Indians 164 & 231, Essex 328/8d & 68/4
Result: Essex won by 6 wickets

INDIANS	FIRST INNINGS		SECOND INNINGS	
S Gavaskar	c Taylor b Boyce	0	st Taylor b Hobbs	55
K Jayantilal	lbw b Lever	0	c Acfield b Boyce	9
A Wadekar(c)	c Taylor b Lever	0	st Taylor b Acfield	51
D Sardesai	c & b East	53	c Fletcher b Acfield	3
G Viswanath	b Lever	0	c Fletcher b Acfield	9
A Mankad	lbw b Acfield	28	c Saville b East	31
E Solkar	c Taylor b East	52	not out	20
S Venkataraghavan	c Taylor b Boyce	9	c Hobbs b East	13
S Kirmani†	c Fletcher b Boyce	10	hit wicket b Hobbs	13
E Prasanna	not out	10	c Ward b Boyce	4
B Chandrasekhar	b Boyce	0	b Lever	1
Extras	(nb 2)	2	(b 9, lb 1, nb 12)	22
Team score		164		231

Fall of wickets 1st innings: 1-0, 2-0, 3-1, 4-3, 5-52, 6-110, 7-131, 8-153, 9-156, 10-164

Fall of wickets 2nd innings: 1-14, 2-40, 3-112, 4-163, 5-182, 6-188, 7-190, 8-209, 9-216, 10-231

Bowling figures	O	M	R	W	O	M	R	W
K Boyce	18.3	7	33	4	15	6	33	2
J Lever	8	2	13	3	11.2	5	24	1
D Acfield	26	8	52	1	16	8	30	3
R Hobbs	21	4	39	0	38	12	73	2
R East	13	4	25	2	28	9	49	2

ESSEX	FIRST INNINGS		SECOND INNINGS	
B Ward	c Jayantilal b Chandrasekhar	55	not out	5
B Francis	c Wadekar b Venkataraghavan	12	run out	3
G Saville	c Wadekar b Chandrasekhar	30	c Wadekar b Venkataraghavan	3
K Fletcher	not out	106	not out	38
G Barker	c & b Chandrasekhar	8		
K Boyce	lbw b Prasanna	28	lbw b Venkataraghavan	15
B Taylor(c) †	b Venkataraghavan	21	b Venkataraghavan	0
R Hobbs	b Venkataraghavan	10		
R East	c Wadekar b Prasanna	9		
J Lever	not out	37		
Extras	(b 2, lb 6, nb 3, w 1)	12	(b 1, lb 3)	4
Team score		328/8d		68/4

Did not bat: D Acfield

Fall of wickets 1st innings: 1-19, 2-95, 3-114, 4-124, 5-167, 6-210, 7-243, 8-277

Fall of wickets 2nd innings: 1-1, 2-6, 3-36, 4-56

Bowling figures	O	M	R	W	O	M	R	W
E Solkar	5	1	5	0	6.1	1	17	0
S Gavaskar	2	0	11	0				
S Venkataraghavan	38	6	100	3	9	1	36	3
E Prasanna	36	11	85	2	1	0	6	0
B Chandrasekhar	41	4	115	3	1	0	5	0
A Mankad	1	1	0	0				

DH Robins' XI vs Indians – India tour of England 1971 – Tour Match

Dates: 30 June – 2 July 1971 (3-day First-Class match)
Venue: The Saffrons, Eastbourne
Toss: Unknown
Scores: DH Robins' XI 228/8d & 258/5d, Indians 305/8d & 132/4
Result: Draw

DH ROBINS' XI	FIRST INNINGS		SECOND INNINGS	
E Russell	c Wadekar b Govindraj	15	lbw b Abid Ali	22
M Smith	c Krishnamurthy b Govindraj	19	c Abid Ali b Govindraj	15
H Ackerman	c Wadekar b Prasanna	39	c Krishnamurthy b Govindraj	80
P Parfitt	b Prasanna	4	b Gavaskar	76
M Mohammad	c Krishnamurthy b Bedi	15	c Govindraj b Mankad	28
R Hutton	c Gavaskar b Bedi	14	not out	9
T Greig	c Jayantilal b Prasanna	27	not out	19
R Swetman†	c Mankad b Prasanna	10		
C Old	not out	35		
K O'Keeffe	not out	35		
Extras	(b 5, lb 9, nb 1)	15	(lb 3, nb 6)	9
Team score		228/ 8d		258/ 5d

Did not bat: D Robins (c)

Fall of wickets 1st innings: 1-22, 2-51, 3-78, 4-87, 5-105, 6-139, 7-148, 8-157

Fall of wickets 2nd innings: 1-40, 2-40, 3-179, 4-224, 5-230

Bowling figures	O	M	R	W	O	M	R	W
D Govindraj	25	11	55	2	21	5	56	2
S Abid Ali	10	2	33	0	15	4	42	1
B Bedi	33	10	64	2	15	0	58	0
E Prasanna	30	13	61	4	12	0	56	0
A Mankad					4	0	25	1
S Gavaskar					3	0	12	1

INDIANS	FIRST INNINGS		SECOND INNINGS	
S Gavaskar	c Swetman b Mohammad	46	not out	55
A Ali Baig	b Greig	22	run out	38
K Jayantilal	b Old	1		
A Wadekar(c)	lbw b Hutton	45	not out	1
A Mankad	c Mohammad b Old	15	b Parfitt	26
G Viswanath	not out	100		
S Abid Ali	b O'Keeffe	40	st Swetman b Parfitt	0
P Krishnamurthy†	c Swetman b O'Keeffe	0		
D Govindraj	c Robins b O'Keeffe	25	c Ackerman b Old	3
E Prasanna	not out	1		
Extras	(lb 3, nb 7)	10	(lb 7, nb 2)	9
Team score		305/ 8d		132/4

Did not bat: B Bedi

Fall of wickets 1st innings: 1-34, 2-35, 3-117, 4-132, 5-144, 6-228, 7-228, 8-290

Fall of wickets 2nd innings: 1-65, 2-71, 3-130, 4-130

Bowling figures	O	M	R	W	O	M	R	W
C Old	25	1	52	2	13	1	59	1
R Hutton	24	5	62	1	9	0	22	0
K O'Keeffe	24	4	71	3	2	1	6	0
M Mohammad	22	4	61	1	4	0	15	0
T Greig	11	1	46	1	4	0	15	0
P Parfitt	5	3	3	0	2	0	6	2

Kent vs Indians – India tour of England 1971 - Tour Match

Dates: 3-6 July 1971 (3-day First-Class match with rest day on 4 July)
Venue: St Lawrence Ground, Canterbury
Toss: Kent, chose to bat
Scores: Kent 394/8d & 176/4d, Indians 163 & 264/7
Result: Draw

KENT	FIRST INNINGS		SECOND INNINGS	
M Denness(c)	lbw b Chandrasekhar	59		
B Luckhurst	c Mankad b Venkataraghavan	118		
D Nicholls	c Abid Ali b Chandrasekhar	8	c sub b Bedi	57
A Ealham	c Baig b Venkataraghavan	20	c Mankad b Venkataraghavan	87
A Knott†	c Kirmani b Venkataraghavan	49		
J Shepherd	c Jayantilal b Bedi	76	not out	4
G Johnson	c & b Bedi	31	run out	13
B Woolmer	c Kirmani b Bedi	27	not out	10
B Julien	not out	1	b Venkataraghavan	0
Extras	(lb 5)	5	(b 4, lb 1)	5
Team score		394/ 8d		176/ 4d

Did not bat: J Dye, N Graham

Fall of wickets 1st innings: 1-125, 2-157, 3-204, 4-209, 5-305, 6-342, 7-385, 8-394

Fall of wickets 2nd innings: 1-35, 2-137, 3-137, 4-168

Bowling figures	O	M	R	W	O	M	R	W
S Abid Ali	11	1	57	0	11	2	37	0
E Solkar	9	0	45	0	10	2	29	0
S Venkataraghavan	37	9	93	3	12	1	47	2
B Bedi	33.4	6	101	3	10	1	26	1
B Chandrasekhar	27	4	93	2	4	0	24	0
A Mankad					2	0	8	0

INDIANS	FIRST INNINGS		SECOND INNINGS	
A Ali Baig	c Knott b Shepherd	58	c Shepherd b Dye	32
K Jayantilal	c Nicholls b Graham	0	b Julien	1
A Mankad	b Graham	6	c Nicholls b Shepherd	52
S Kirmani†	b Graham	17	not out	4
D Sardesai	b Dye	5	c Nicholls b Shepherd	0
G Viswanath	b Dye	0	not out	115
E Solkar	not out	50	c Knott b Graham	32
S Abid Ali	c Knott b Woolmer	2	c Shepherd b Graham	13
S Venkataraghavan(c)	c Knott b Shepherd	6	b Nicholls	0
B Bedi	c Denness b Shepherd	6		
B Chandrasekhar	c Julien b Shepherd	6		
Extras	(lb 3, nb 4)	7	(lb 11, nb 4)	15
Team score		163		264/7

Fall of wickets 1st innings: 1-0, 2-14, 3-40, 4-52, 5-52, 6-112, 7-121, 8-145, 9-155, 10-163

Fall of wickets 2nd innings: 1-53, 2-146, 3-146, 4-196, 5-231, 6-248, 7-250

Bowling figures	O	M	R	W		O	M	R	W
J Dye	13	2	39	2		13	5	34	1
N Graham	17	4	60	3		28	11	57	2
B Woolmer	12	5	20	1		5	2	4	0
J Shepherd	10.1	2	33	4		18	7	41	2
G Johnson	1	0	4	0		31	12	53	0
B Julien						18	7	43	1
B Luckhurst						7	2	17	0
D Nicholls						1	1	0	1

Engineer Breaks Curfew

Colonel Hemu Adhikari, the Indian manager for the tour to England in 1971, had a military-like approach to keep the team in check. On the sojourn, he kept a close eye on all the players, famously imposing a curfew for the team – which entailed every member being in bed by 10.30pm. Adhikari would then personally go around to check if the players had followed his instructions. Farokh Engineer, who lived in England then and wanted to have a night out, came up with an ingenious plan to beat Adhikari's rules.

One of Adhikari's policies was that each room would be shared by a junior and a senior – in order to allow the youngsters the opportunity to learn from the established stars. Engineer was rooming with his understudy, Syed Kirmani, who was on his first tour with the Indian team. As Adhikari's cut-off time dawned, Engineer set a few pillows on his bed and covered it with a blanket. He then asked Kirmani to switch off the lights and when the Colonel came around, only to open the door slightly, so that he doesn't get a complete look inside[87].

At 10:30pm, there was a knock on the door. Kirmani turned off the lights and opened the door to find Adhikari. "He (Adhikari) put his head in and said, 'so raha hai, ja tu bhi soja' (Hindi for: He is sleeping. You go to sleep as well). I closed the door and went to

---

87   Wadekar's Warriors. Accessed at: https://youtu.be/ATVNi2CFEfE (At: 2:48:47)

bed," Kirmani recalled[88]. Engineer returned early in the morning and went to bed. He managed to sneak out without arousing any suspicion – with a little help from the man who eventually succeeded him for India.

88 I started off by using a brick as gloves: Kirmani, The Times of India, Published on May 17, 2002. Accessed at: https://timesofindia.indiatimes.com/sports/new-zealand-in-india-2016/interviews/I-started-off-by-using-a-brick-as-gloves-Kirmani/articleshow/10351150.cms

Farokh Engineer missed out on the West Indies tour but was brought back for the Tests in England. With good experience of playing in English conditions, he was crucial to India's campaign.

Gavaskar the Bowler

At a time when India's bowling approach was dominated by spin, the new ball was an unwanted burden for there weren't many who could exploit it. As noted earlier, Syed Abid Ali and Eknath Solkar, the medium pacers, were mainly tasked with the responsibility of taking the shine off the ball. Apart from these all-rounders, India also found other men to do the needful, for example, wicketkeeper-batsman Budhi Kunderan did it at Birmingham in 1967 – in the only Test where India fielded the entire spin quartet. Sunil Gavaskar, India's great opening batsman, also had the enviable task of taking the shine off a few times. In 29 Test innings with the ball, he opened the bowling on five occasions and was brought in first change twice.

On Test debut in the Caribbean, Gavaskar had bowled an over in the first innings. Rohan Kanhai, the West Indian No. 3, faced him up and hit a boundary. "I bowled slightly short and he square-cut me for a boundary. Typically like all fast-bowlers, my next ball was a bouncer and he didn't expect it because god he'd played much faster bowlers. But he ducked under it because there was no problem and just laughed. He had this 'What is this guy doing bowling a bouncer to me?' look. He looked at me and laughed," Gavaskar said[89]. "One of my day-dreams was Rohan Kanhai caught behind off my outswinger," said Gavaskar, who in a way had a few bowling ambitions.

---

89 Sunny Days Feat Sunil Gavaskar, 22 Yarns, Gaurav Kapoor, Spotify.

On India's tour to England in 1971, Ajit Wadekar used the young Gavaskar's bowling skills on more than an occasion – at times to get a breakthrough. To Wadekar's good fortune, it worked on a couple of occasions. In one tour game against Leicestershire, Wadekar summoned Gavaskar to help him get rid of the doughty Roger Tolchard. "You talk about your leg-spinners. Here, have a go, but it will be just one over," Wadekar said as he handed the ball to Gavaskar[90]. Immediately, Gavaskar dismissed Tolchard with an innocuous ball, as the captain completed the catch at slip.

Gavaskar picked a total of four First-Class wickets on the tour, which included a spell of two for eight against Hampshire. In the second Test at Old Trafford, he even sent down 12 overs in the second essay.

---

90   My Cricketing Years, Ajit Wadekar as told to KN Prabhu, p. 97. Published by Vikas Publishing House Pvt Ltd 1973

Leicestershire vs Indians – India tour of England 1971 – Tour Match

Dates: 7-9 July 1971 (3-day First-Class match)
Venue: Grace Road, Leicester
Toss: Leicestershire, chose to bat
Scores: Leicestershire 198 & 168, Indians 416/7d
Result: Indians won by an innings & 50 runs

LEICESTERSHIRE	FIRST INNINGS		SECOND INNINGS	
B Dudleston	run out	51	b Chandrasekhar	8
J Steele	c & b Chandrasekhar	26	lbw b Chandrasekhar	22
C Balderstone	c Wadekar b Prasanna	15	lbw b Venkataraghavan	63
C Inman	c K'murthy b Venkataraghavan	49	c Solkar b Chandrasekhar	11
B Davison	c Solkar b Prasanna	13	c Gavaskar b Chandrasekhar	0
R Tolchard(c) †	b Chandrasekhar	6	c Wadekar b Gavaskar	30
J Birkenshaw	c V'raghavan b Chandrasekhar	3	c Krishnamurthy b Chandrasekhar	6
G Cross	c & b Chandrasekhar	19	c Krishnamurthy b Venkataraghavan	0
G McKenzie	c Gavaskar b Chandrasekhar	1	c Gavaskar b Chandrasekhar	5
T Spencer	b Venkataraghavan	10	c sub b Venkataraghavan	6
R Matthews	not out	0	not out	1
Extras	(lb 5)	5	(b 10, lb 2, nb 4)	16
Team score		198		168

Fall of wickets 1st innings: 1-60, 2-85, 3-121, 4-142, 5-163, 6-163, 7-170, 8-178, 9-198, 10-198

Fall of wickets 2nd innings: 1-24, 2-54, 3-66, 4-66, 5-138, 6-152, 7-152, 8-152, 9-162, 10-168

Bowling figures	O	M	R	W	O	M	R	W
D Govindraj	8	3	31	0	2	0	9	0
E Solkar	5	0	18	0	6	1	20	0
E Prasanna	21	7	42	2	16	8	21	0
B Chandrasekhar	21.2	4	63	5	28	9	64	6
S Venkataraghavan	18	5	39	2	19	6	31	3
S Gavaskar					2	1	7	1

INDIANS	FIRST INNINGS	
S Gavaskar	c Tolchard b Matthews	165
A Ali Baig	c & b Birkenshaw	23
A Wadekar(c)	c Birkenshaw b Steele	126
D Sardesai	b Birkenshaw	1
A Mankad	not out	43
E Solkar	c Davison b Birkenshaw	12
S Venkataraghavan	run out	38
D Govindraj	run out	0
Extras	(lb 2, nb 5, w 1)	8
Team score		416/7d

Did not bat: E Prasanna, B Chandrasekhar, P Krishnamurthy†

Fall of wickets 1-46, 2-277, 3-278, 4-339, 5-363, 6-415, 7-416

Bowling figures	O	M	R	W
G McKenzie	13	2	56	0
R Matthews	16	3	58	1
J Birkenshaw	45	6	128	3
C Balderstone	6	2	13	0
G Cross	12	1	36	0
T Spencer	10	2	29	0
J Steele	22	5	70	1
B Dudleston	6	0	18	0

John Jameson on the Indian Radar

John Jameson was born in 1941 in Bombay to English parents, who lived a large part of their lives in India. Jameson grew up in Bombay and attended the Cathedral and John Connon School. A few years after India's independence, a teenaged Jameson travelled back to England, where he started making a name as a cricketer. In the 1960s, he established himself in the Warwickshire side, becoming a regular in county cricket with some stable performances.

It was the year 1970 and India weren't playing Test cricket that year but had a packed schedule for the following year. The Indian selectors got word of Jameson and his Indian birth, and explored the possibility of having him open the batting the following year. A message was sent across to Jameson that he should contact the Indian board if he considered the possibility of playing for India. "No one ever approached me. I was informed by one of the England selectors that India have made enquiries," he said in an interview years later[91]. Jameson entertained the thought but chose England despite the fact that his parents continued to live in India. His loyalties clearly stayed with England.

---

91   Nagraj Gollapudi, Cricinfo, From Byculla to The Oval, and back. Published on 03-12-2009. Accessed at: https://www.espncricinfo.com/story/john-jameson-s-india-connection-437869

Ironically, when India played Warwickshire on their 1971 tour, Jameson smashed 231 against the country of his birth. Geoff Boycott did not feature after the first Test against India and that opened up a berth at the top for Jameson. In the first innings of the third Test at The Oval, he recorded his highest Test score of 82. In all he played four Tests and three One-Day Internationals (ODIs) for England. In 1975, he was also a part of England's squad for the inaugural World Cup.

Coincidentally, on India's forgettable tour to England in 1974, Jameson pummelled two centuries in one game against the tourists, while playing for the DH Robins' XI.

Warwickshire vs Indians – India tour of England 1971 - Tour Match

Dates: 10-13 July 1971 (3-day First-Class match with rest day on 11 July)
Venue: Edgbaston, Birmingham
Toss: Warwickshire, chose to bat
Scores: Warwickshire 377/3d & 182, Indians 562
Result: Indians won by an innings & 3 runs

WARWICKSHIRE	FIRST INNINGS		SECOND INNINGS	
J Whitehouse	st Krishnamurthy b Bedi	52	c Krishnamurthy b Bedi	25
J Jameson	lbw b Bedi	231	c Bedi b Abid Ali	11
R Kanhai	c Abid Ali b Bedi	4	c & b Bedi	59
M Smith	not out	72	c & b Bedi	38
E Hemmings	lbw b Prasanna	9		
B Ibadulla	not out	13		
B Blenkiron	c Prasanna b Bedi	1		
A Smith(c)†	c Gavaskar b Prasanna	3		
P Lewington	lbw b Prasanna	10		
P Dunkels	c Gavaskar b Bedi	0		
W Tidy	c sub b Prasanna	0		
Extras	(b 7, lb 10, nb 1)	18	(b 5, lb 6, nb 2)	13
Team score		377/ 3d		182

Fall of wickets 1st innings: 1-132, 2-136, 3-377

Fall of wickets 2nd innings: 1-28, 2-64, 3-132, 4-149, 5-151, 6-152, 7-160, 8-178, 9-179, 10-182

Bowling figures	O	M	R	W	O	M	R	W
D Govindraj	12	2	50	0	3	0	21	0
S Abid Ali	15	2	74	0	10	1	20	1
E Solkar	5	0	33	0				
B Bedi	22	3	106	3	37	13	64	5
E Prasanna	26	3	96	0	30.2	9	57	4
S Gavaskar					1	0	7	0

INDIANS	INNINGS	
S Gavaskar	c Jameson b Blenkiron	25
A Ali Baig	c Jameson b Blenkiron	32
A Wadekar(c)	c Jameson b Lewington	77
D Sardesai	b Ibadulla	120
G Viswanath	c & b Jameson	90
E Solkar	c Hemmings b Jameson	35
S Abid Ali	b Blenkiron	93
P Krishnamurthy†	c Jameson b Blenkiron	32
D Govindraj	b Blenkiron	7
E Prasanna	lbw b Ibadulla	10
B Bedi	not out	6
Extras	(b 12, lb 6, nb 17)	35
Team score		562

Fall of wickets 1-50, 2-70, 3-214, 4-332, 5-388, 6-421, 7-525, 8-537, 9-553, 10-562

Bowling figures	O	M	R	W
B Blenkiron	30.1	4	100	5
P Dunkels	25	2	91	0
E Hemmings	25	5	67	0
W Tidy	32	4	124	0
P Lewington	16	5	34	1
B Ibadulla	15	6	23	2
J Jameson	19	2	76	2
A Smith	2	0	12	0

Glamorgan vs Indians – India tour of England 1971 - Tour Match

Dates: 14-16 July 1971 (3-day First-Class match)
Venue: Sophia Gardens, Cardiff
Toss: Indians, chose to bat
Scores: Indians 284 & 245/6d, Glamorgan 203 & 224
Result: Indians won by 102 runs

INDIANS	FIRST INNINGS		SECOND INNINGS	
S Gavaskar	c Nash b Walker	39	lbw b Fredericks	14
A Ali Baig	c Lyons b Khan	47	b Khan	28
A Wadekar(c)	c Walker b Khan	1	run out	73
G Viswanath	c Khan b Fredericks	52	c A Jones b Walker	5
S Abid Ali	st E Jones b Fredericks	46	not out	16
F Engineer	not out	62	c Walker b Fredericks	28
S Venkataraghavan	c A Jones b Cordle	12	c E Jones b Williams	57
S Kirmani†	b Cordle	5		
D Govindraj	b Cordle	2	not out	6
B Bedi	c Nash b Cordle	0		
B Chandrasekhar	c Fredericks b Williams	1		
Extras	(b 4, lb 9, nb 4)	17	(b 10, lb 4, nb 4)	18
Team score		284		245/ 6d

Fall of wickets 1st innings: 1-71, 2-72, 3-99, 4-188, 5-207, 6-234, 7-242, 8-271, 9-271, 10-284

Fall of wickets 2nd innings: 1-45, 2-46, 3-60, 4-106, 5-206, 6-239

Bowling figures	O	M	R	W	O	M	R	W
M Nash	7	2	21	0	2	0	6	0
L Williams	17	2	46	1	10	1	58	1
T Cordle	13	3	49	4	9	4	18	0
P Walker	33	15	54	1	25	6	74	1
M Khan	23	10	49	2	16	5	39	1
M Llewellyn	1	0	3	0				
R Fredericks	10	2	45	2	9	1	32	2

GLAMORGAN	FIRST INNINGS		SECOND INNINGS	
A Jones	c Kirmani b Venkataraghavan	26	c Wadekar b Bedi	55
K Lyons	c Baig b Bedi	35	c Abid Ali b Bedi	0
M Khan	b Bedi	78	c & b Venkataraghavan	8
R Fredericks	c & b Venkataraghavan	15	b Bedi	5
P Walker	c Baig b Venkataraghavan	26	c Baig b Venkataraghavan	44
T Lewis(c)	b Bedi	0	b Bedi	21
E Jones†	b Venkataraghavan	9	lbw b Bedi	2
T Cordle	c Wadekar b Venkataraghavan	4	c sub b Venkataraghavan	4
M Nash	c & b Venkataraghavan	1	c Viswanath b Bedi	75
M Llewellyn	retired ill	0	absent ill	
L Williams	not out	0	not out	0
Extras	(b 4, lb 5)	9	(b 8, lb 2)	10
Team score		203		224

Fall of wickets 1st innings: 1-54, 2-111, 3-142, 4-178, 5-184, 6-190, 7-194, 8-202, 9-203

Fall of wickets 2nd innings: 1-49, 2-95, 3-116, 4-117, 5-198, 6-203, 7-205, 8-224, 9-224

Bowling figures	O	R	M	W	O	M	R	W
D Govindraj	3	1	12	0	1	0	10	0
S Abid Ali	4	1	9	0	3	1	8	0
B Bedi	19	5	66	3	39.2	8	93	6
B Chandrasekhar	17	8	31	0				
S Venkataraghavan	25.2	7	76	6	37	6	97	3
S Kirmani					2	0	6	0

Hampshire vs Indians – India tour of England 1971 - Tour Match

Dates: 17-20 July 1971 (3-day First-Class match with rest day on 18 July)
Venue: Dean Park, Bournemouth
Toss: Hampshire, chose to bat
Scores: Hampshire 198 & 271, Indians 364 & 106/5
Result: Indians won by 5 wickets

HAMPSHIRE	FIRST INNINGS		SECOND INNINGS	
B Richards	c & b Solkar	10	st Krishnamurthy b Venkataraghavan	45
R Lewis	c Krishnamurthy b Prasanna	28	c Krishnamurthy b Venkataraghavan	71
D Turner	lbw b Govindraj	0	c Solkar b Venkataraghavan	11
R Gilliat(c)	run out	50	st Krishnamurthy b Venkataraghavan	79
D Livingstone	c Viswanath b Prasanna	44	c Gavaskar b Venkataraghavan	9
T Jesty	b Venkataraghavan	5	not out	11
B Stephenson†	c Sardesai b Gavaskar	27	c Solkar b Venkataraghavan	15
J Holder	c Sardesai b Prasanna	5	c Gavaskar b Venkataraghavan	0
D O'Sullivan	not out	25	lbw b Venkataraghavan	4
L Worrell	c & b Govindraj	2	b Solkar	16
B White	lbw b Gavaskar	1	c Baig b Venkataraghavan	0
Extras	(lb 1)	1	(b 7, lb 3)	10
Team score		198		271

Fall of wickets 1st innings: 1-13, 2-22, 3-59, 4-101, 5-114, 6-144, 7-161, 8-188, 9-195, 10-198

Fall of wickets 2nd innings: 1-73, 2-113, 3-173, 4-195, 5-225, 6-231, 7-231, 8-252, 9-270, 10-271

Bowling figures	O	M	R	W		O	M	R	W
D Govindraj	10	2	43	2		6	1	15	0
E Solkar	13	4	33	1		17	4	47	1
E Prasanna	27	9	37	3		33	6	81	0
S Venkataraghavan	22	5	76	1		36.3	13	93	9
S Gavaskar	1.3	0	8	2		3	0	25	0
A Wadekar						1	1	0	0

INDIANS	FIRST INNINGS		SECOND INNINGS	
S Gavaskar	c Livingstone b O'Sullivan	53	c Richards b O'Sullivan	25
A Ali Baig	c O'Sullivan b White	4	b Holder	2
A Mankad	c Gilliat b Worrell	109		
D Sardesai	c Holder b O'Sullivan	12	c & b O'Sullivan	4
G Viswanath	st Stephenson b O'Sullivan	122		
A Wadekar(c)	b Worrell	20	c Worrell b O'Sullivan	27
E Solkar	c Richards b Worrell	5	not out	7
S Venkataraghavan	c Stephenson b O'Sullivan	7	c & b Worrell	19
P Krishnamurthy†	c & b O'Sullivan	2		
D Govindraj	c Gilliat b Worrell	6	not out	15
E Prasanna	not out	7		
Extras	(b 2, lb 4, nb 10, w 1)	17	(lb 3, nb 4)	7
Team score		364		106/5

Fall of wickets 1st innings: 1-13, 2-97, 3-125, 4-268, 5-304, 6-342, 7-342, 8-345, 9-352, 10-364

Fall of wickets 2nd innings: 1-4, 2-54, 3-63, 4-72, 5-94

Bowling figures	O	M	R	W		O	M	R	W
B White	21	10	46	1		5	1	13	0
J Holder	23	5	57	0		6	1	12	1
L Worrell	49	18	102	4		12	1	47	1
D O'Sullivan	54.4	18	116	5		10	1	27	3
B Richards	5	2	8	0					
D Turner	5	1	18	0					

Indian Team Meets Queen at Lord's

During the first Test at Lord's, Queen Elizabeth II made an appearance at one of the tea breaks to meet and greet the two teams. As a tradition, the Queen would come to the hallowed turf, meet the teams at the break, watch the game for a while and then leave to attend to her other duties. As the Queen walked out to meet the teams, the Indians lined up with the captain, Ajit Wadekar, handling the duty of introducing all his players to royalty.

However, the Indians had no idea as to how to greet or courtesy the Queen. "Nobody told us how to shake hands or what to do, what to say or what not to say," Kenia Jayantilal recalled.

The Queen possibly had an idea of the visitor's cluelessness. "When I shook hands she asked me, 'This is your first visit?' I said yes this is my first visit to England," said Jayantilal[92].

Back in 1967, the Queen had met the Indian team during their Test match at Lord's. A few members of that side were present in 1971 as well.

---

92 Conversation with the author

Wadekar Stands up to Snow

Captain Ajit Wadekar had set the tone in the Caribbean by standing up to Uton Dowe despite an injured hand in the first tour game. In England, he replicated a similar performance, this time in the first Test at Lord's. Fast bowler John Snow was at his peak and had made waves in the Ashes during the previous Australian summer. With 31 wickets in the Ashes, Snow had troubled the Australians with his pace and had infamously felled Terry Jenner with a rising delivery at Sydney. Hailed as one of the best fast bowlers in the world, the Indians were facing a challenge.

During the first innings at Lord's, Wadekar took on Snow head on, fearlessly hooking the paceman's bouncers. "I walked in at one down and he naturally started bouncing me. I hooked his first four bouncers for fours, and he stopped bowling me bouncers. That's what made everyone realise, 'Okay, even John Snow, on his home-grown green wicket can also be played'," Wadekar said[93].

By the time the skipper was dismissed with India's score on 125, he had accounted for a remarkable 85 out of those. It was an encore

---

93   When Ajit Wadekar Reminisced The Summer of '71. BCCI Official Website. Published on August 16, 2018. Accessed at: https://www.bcci.tv/articles/2018/news/99893/when-ajit-wadekar-reminisced-the-summer-of-71

of Jamaica! While India did not win the Test match, the captain led from the front and dispelled fears of Snow's dominance. "The 85 I scored in that innings against Snow and Co was certainly one of my best knocks," he later recalled[94].

---

94 Ajit Wadekar, When One And One Made Eleven, 75 Years of Indian Cricket, Outlook Cricket Special 2004, p 71

'Go and Tell Your Aunty'

Eknath Solkar got the better of Geoffrey Boycott on India's torrid tour to England in 1974 but perhaps the seeds of that tussle were sown during the previous visit. During the second innings of the first Test at Lord's, the England opener had got his eye in and moved to 33, while building a solid stand with John Edrich. Ajit Wadekar summoned his deputy S Venkataraghavan to get the breakthrough.

Wadekar placed Solkar at short-leg and took his spot around leg-slip. Boycott had hit Venkataraghavan for two fours before he flicked one to the leg-side. The ball ricochet off Solkar's leg and lobbed to Wadekar, who completed the catch. Boycott couldn't quite believe what had transpired and was looking around. Solkar then told Boycott, "Go and tell your aunty." The England opener then walked back to the pavillion.

Wadekar asked Solkar about his jibe at Boycott. "That is because his girlfriend is elder to him," Solkar explained[95].

95 Dwarkanath Sanzgiri's YouTube Channel. Tribute to Eknath Solkar. Accessed at: https://www.youtube.com/watch?v=c1lOmxo0_SM (At 21:00)

Weatherman's Word Makes India Go for the Target

On Day Five of the first Test at Lord's, England resumed their second innings at 145 for five with some rain in the offing. S Venkataraghavan and Bhagwat Chandrasekhar combined to take the last five wickets to bowl England out for 191. India were up against a target of 183 and had over four hours to get them. Eventually, India made a dash and showed all the intent to get there. However, the heavens gave way at 145 for eight around tea time. Both sides went into the famed pavillion at Lord's thinking they had a shot at victory.

India's decision to make a dash towards the target was taken after the captain had a word with weathermen. "I had already consulted the weather bureau and ordered the batsmen to take a chance because rain was forecast in the afternoon. Otherwise, we had all the time to score the 183 needed for victory," Ajit Wadekar said[96].

India's intentions were evident when they sent the belligerent Farokh Engineer at 21 for two. Along with Sunil Gavaskar, Engineer took India to 87 before wickets fell at regular intervals. Emotions fluctuated as India were first expected to win and then the rain rescued them from a possible defeat.

---

96 Sunder Rajan, India vs England 1971, Published by Jaico Publishing House. Second Impression 1972. P. 39

John Snow Barges Into Sunil Gavaskar

On the final day of the first Test at Lord's, both teams felt the pressure to go for a win. Chasing 183 with a little over four hours to play and with rain on the anvil, India made a dash towards the target. Sensing India's charge, England too fancied their chances of getting a few wickets to push the initiative. At 21 for two, Farokh Engineer joined Sunil Gavaskar in the middle and they then constructed a useful partnership.

With lunch in sight, Engineer tapped one onto the leg-side from John Snow – England's premier fast bowler. Gavaskar responded to his partner's call and tried to scamper across for a quick single. Snow ran across to gather the ball but barged into Gavaskar, who tumbled onto the ground. "I was trying to get to the ball first to run Sunny out. I was expecting Sunny to run over the top of the ball. In order to get to the ball, I made a desperate effort. We got into a tangle, and ended up in a big heap," Snow later said[97]. Once Gavaskar got up, Snow even picked up his bat and tossed it across to him. The whole episode left a sour taste in the mouth as the members of the Marylebone Cricket Club (MCC) watched on from the famed pavillion.

---

97 S Dinakar, John Snow: This Snow is still full of fire. Sportstar. Published on: March 6, 1993. Accessed at: https://sportstar.thehindu.com/cricket/sportstar-archives-interview-john-snow-england-cricket-australia-ashes-india-sunil-gavaskar/article31604563.ece

Snow said, "As I made contact and Gavaskar started to fall, I could sense the shocked silence in the MCC committee room. I knew I was going to be in trouble." The matter did not end there as the Test and County Cricket Board (TCCB) secretary walked into the England dressing room at lunch and expressed his disgust[98]. Alec Bedser, the chairman of England's selectors, asked Snow to apologise to Gavaskar. However, the fast bowler was disturbed by the number of people who had descended upon the dressing room and did not apologise during the break. Instead, Snow had a small chat with Gavaskar on the field.

While the matter was dead and buried for the Indian team, the English differed and Snow was axed for the second Test on disciplinary grounds.

---

98 Martin Williamson, Snow and Sunny's argy bargy. Cricinfo. Published on: August 11, 2007. Accessed at: https://www.espncricinfo.com/story/snow-and-sunny-s-argy-bargy-306544

John Snow had made his mark during the Ashes in 1970-71 in Australia. The leader of England's pace attack, Snow found himself axed for the second Test at Manchester following the collision with Sunil Gavaskar at Lord's.

England vs India – 1st Test – India tour of England 1971

Dates: 22-27 July 1971 (5-day Test match with rest day on 25 July)
Venue: Lord's, London
Toss: England, chose to bat
Scores: ENG 304 & 191, IND 313 & 145/8
Result: Draw
Series status: 0-0

ENGLAND	FIRST INNINGS		SECOND INNINGS	
G Boycott	c Engineer b Abid Ali	3	c Wadekar b Venkataraghavan	33
B Luckhurst	c Solkar b Chandrasekhar	30	b Solkar	1
J Edrich	c Venkataraghavan b Bedi	18	c Engineer b Bedi	62
D Amiss	c Engineer b Bedi	9	run out	0
B D'Oliveira	c Solkar b Chandrasekhar	4	b Bedi	30
A Knott†	c Wadekar b Venkataraghavan	67	c Wadekar b Chandrasekhar	24
R Illingworth(c)	c Engineer b Bedi	33	c Wadekar b Venkataraghavan	20
R Hutton	b Venkataraghavan	20	b Chandrasekhar	0
J Snow	c Abid Ali b Chandrasekhar	73	c Chandrasekhar b Venkataraghavan	9
N Gifford	b Bedi	17	not out	7
J Price	not out	5	c Abid Ali b Venkataraghavan	0
Extras	(b 8, lb 12, nb 5)	25	(lb 5)	5
Team score		304		191

Fall of wickets: 1st innings: 1-18, 2-46, 3-56, 4-61, 5-71, 6-161, 7-183, 8-223, 9-294, 10-304

Fall of wickets: 2nd innings: 1-4, 2-65, 3-70, 4-117, 5-145, 6-153, 7-153, 8-174, 9-189, 10-191

Bowling figures	O	M	R	W	O	M	R	W
S Abid Ali	15	3	38	1	9	1	20	0
E Solkar	8	3	17	0	6	3	13	1
S Venkataraghavan	28	8	44	2	30.5	11	52	4
B Chandrasekhar	49	10	110	3	23	7	60	2
B Bedi	39.3	18	70	4	30	13	41	2

INDIA	FIRST INNINGS		SECOND INNINGS	
A Mankad	c Gifford b Snow	1	c Knott b Snow	5
S Gavaskar	c Amiss b Price	4	c Edrich b Gifford	53
A Wadekar (c)	c Illingworth b Gifford	85	c Boycott b Price	5
D Sardesai	c Illingworth b Gifford	25	b Illingworth	1
G Viswanath	c Knott b Hutton	68	c Amiss b Gifford	9
F Engineer†	c Illingworth b Hutton	28	st Knott b Gifford	35
E Solkar	c Knott b Gifford	67	not out	6
S Abid Ali	c Luckhurst b Snow	6	c Snow b Illingworth	14
S Venkataraghavan	c Hutton b Price	11	c Hutton b Gifford	7
B Bedi	c Price b Gifford	0	not out	2
B Chandrasekhar	not out	0		
Extras	(b 7, lb 9, nb 2)	18	(lb 7, nb 1)	8
Team score		313		145/8

Fall of wickets: 1st innings: 1-1, 2-29, 3-108, 4-125, 5-175, 6-267, 7-279, 8-302, 9-311, 10-313

Fall of wickets: 2nd innings: 1-8, 2-21, 3-87, 4-101, 5-108, 6-114, 7-135, 8-142

Bowling figures	O	M	R	W	O	M	R	W
J Price	25	9	46	2	4	0	26	1
J Snow	31	9	64	2	8	0	23	1
R Hutton	24	8	38	2	3	0	12	0
N Gifford	45.3	14	84	4	19	4	43	4
B D'Oliveira	15	7	20	0				
R Illingworth	25	12	43	0	16	2	33	2

Minor Counties vs Indians – India tour of England 1971 - Tour Match

Dates: 28-30 July 1971 (3-day First-Class match)
Venue: County Ground, Lakenham
Toss: Minor Counties, chose to bat
Scores: Minor Counties 203/5d & 199/6d, Indians 252/3d & 26/0
Result: Draw

MINOR COUNTIES	FIRST INNINGS		SECOND INNINGS	
G Robinson†	b Chandrasekhar	35	c & b Venkataraghavan	29
A Sutton	c Kirmani b Govindraj	29	lbw b Govindraj	0
R Cox	b Chandrasekhar	24	retired hurt	0
P Shippey	c Sardesai b Venkataraghavan	10	b Chandrasekhar	19
M Maslin	c Sardesai b Chandrasekhar	61	c Govindraj b Chandrasekhar	18
F Millett(c)	not out	24	not out	50
G Hunter	not out	9	c Mankad b Solkar	41
G Ridley	b Mankad	35		
G Jarrett	not out	2		
Extras	(b 2, lb 9)	11	(b 1, lb 3, nb 1)	5
Team score		203/ 5d		199/ 6d

Did not bat – P Timmis, P Dunkels

Fall of wickets 1st innings: 1-56, 2-79, 3-98, 4-106, 5-194

Fall of wickets 2nd innings: 1-3, 2-44, 3-48, 4-77, 5-154, 6-197

Bowling figures	O	M	R	W	O	M	R	W
D Govindraj	10	2	43	1	6	2	14	1
S Abid Ali	8	0	40	0	5	1	16	0
S Venkataraghavan	18	2	41	1	12	2	29	1
B Chandrasekhar	19	3	39	3	15	2	30	2
E Solkar	4	1	16	0	13	2	43	1
S Gavaskar	3	0	13	0	9	0	47	0
D Sardesai					2	0	7	0
A Mankad					1	0	8	1

INDIANS	FIRST INNINGS		SECOND INNINGS	
A Mankad	run out	63		
S Gavaskar	run out	54		
A Ali Baig	b Ridley	64		
D Sardesai	not out	16		
E Solkar	not out	44		
S Kirmani†			not out	13
K Jayantilal			not out	8
Extras	(b 4, lb 2, nb 4, w 1)	11	(b 4, nb 1)	5
Team score		252/3d		26/0

Did not bat –S Abid Ali, S Venkataraghavan (c), D Govindraj, B Chandrasekhar

Fall of wickets 1st innings: 1-87, 2-191, 3-191

Bowling figures	O	M	R	W	O	M	R	W
P Timmis	7	1	27	0	5	2	9	0
P Dunkels	10	2	34	0	2	0	6	0
G Hunter	15	4	52	0				
G Ridley	18	7	59	1				
G Jarrett	14	2	47	0	3	2	6	0
A Sutton	10	2	22	0				
M Maslin					1	1	0	0

Surrey vs Indians – India tour of England 1971 - Tour Match

Dates: 31 July – 2 August 1971 (3-day First-Class match)
Venue: The Oval, London
Toss: Surrey, chose to bat
Scores: Surrey 269 & 257/4, Indians 326/8d
Result: Draw

SURREY	FIRST INNINGS		SECOND INNINGS	
J Edrich	c Baig b Abid Ali	1	c Wadekar b Prasanna	23
R Lewis	run out	18	st Krishnamurthy b Prasanna	36
M Stewart(c)	c Krishnamurthy b Bedi	24	c Abid Ali b Prasanna	45
Y Ahmed	C Jayantilal b Bedi	52	c Krishnamurthy b Prasanna	16
G Roope	c Sardesai b Bedi	60	not out	56
S Storey	c Wadekar b Bedi	2	not out	70
I Alam	c Krishnamurthy b Bedi	55		
A Long†	c Jayantilal b Bedi	10		
P Pocock	st Krishnamurthy b Prasanna	28		
G Arnold	b Bedi	0		
B Willis	not out	9		
Extras	(b 2, lb 3, nb 4, w 1)	10	(b 6, lb 4, nb 1)	11
Team score		269		257/4

Fall of wickets 1st innings: 1-2, 2-39, 3-70, 4-131, 5-139, 6-202, 7-226, 8-259, 9-259, 10-269

Fall of wickets 2nd innings: 1-39, 2-96, 3-125, 4-130

Bowling figures	O	M	R	W	O	M	R	W
D Govindraj	12	1	32	0	8	3	12	0
S Abid Ali	8	2	21	1	4	2	6	0
E Prasanna	32.1	5	89	1	26	4	69	4
B Bedi	37	11	111	7	24	9	46	0
A Mankad	2	1	6	0	12	2	42	0
D Sardesai					3	0	7	0
K Jayantilal					5	0	15	0
A Wadekar					5	0	25	0
A Ali Baig					4	0	24	0

INDIANS	FIRST INNINGS	
A Mankad	c Long b Storey	77
K Jayantilal	run out	84
A Wadekar(c)	b Arnold	3
D Sardesai	b Arnold	13
G Viswanath	c Roope b Willis	39
A Ali Baig	b Willis	21
S Abid Ali	b Storey	34
P Krishnamurthy†	b Willis	5
D Govindraj	not out	28
B Bedi	not out	1
Extras	(b 1, lb 15, nb 4, w 1)	21
Team score		326/8d

Did not bat: E Prasanna

Fall of wickets 1-129, 2-132, 3-152, 4-231, 5-233, 6-259, 7-273, 8-314

Bowling figures	O	M	R	W
G Arnold	31	6	77	2
B Willis	27	8	75	3
P Pocock	27	11	67	0
I Alam	20	8	45	0
S Storey	19	6	41	2

Peter Lever Misses Out on Double Honours

Peter Lever was drafted into the England side in place of John Snow, who was dropped following his shoulder-clash with Sunil Gavaskar at Lord's. It was a special occasion for Lever, a Lancastrian, as he got an opportunity to represent his country at his home ground Old Trafford, Manchester and he was determined to make it count. Batting first, England were in trouble at 187 for seven when Lever joined his captain Ray Illingworth in the middle. In tandem, they rescued England with a 168-run partnership before the England captain was dismissed for 107.

Lever carried on, sensing an opportunity to score a Test century but only had Nos 10 and 11 for company. Norman Gifford hung around to help Lever into the 80s until he was dismissed by Eknath Solkar. John Price, the last man walked out, but was run out soon after, leaving Lever stranded on 88 not out. "It was my own fault," Lever later confessed. "I smacked one and someone fielded it really well. I tried to turn round, he tried to turn round but slipped on his backside," Lever said describing the moment[99].

---

99 Scott Oliver, 'If I could do it all again, I'd gamble more' – Peter Lever. The Cricket Monthly. Published on November 15, 2013. Accessed at: https://www.thecricketmonthly.com/story/688625/-if-i-could-do-it-all-again--i-d-gamble-more

186 | Twice upon a Time

However, he made up for the disappointment by taking a five-wicket haul in India's first innings. Had he completed his century, Lever would have had the pleasure of seeing his name on the batting and bowling honour's boards at Old Trafford. This Test match also remains his only appearance for England at his home ground.

India were bowled out for 212 in reply, with Sunil Gavaskar scoring 57 and Eknath Solkar getting 50. Brian Luckhurst's 101 powered England to 245 for three in the second innings. Chasing 420, India ended Day Four on 65 for three and no play was possible on the final day due to rain. India got out of jail here!

England vs India – 2nd Test – India tour of England 1971

Dates: 5-10 August 1971 (5-day Test match with rest day on 8 August)
Venue: Old Trafford, Manchester
Toss: England, chose to bat
Scores: ENG 386 & 245/3d, IND 212 & 65/3
Result: Draw
Series status: 0-0

ENGLAND	FIRST INNINGS		SECOND INNINGS	
B Luckhurst	c Viswanath b Bedi	78	st Engineer b Solkar	101
J Jameson	c Gavaskar b Abid Ali	15	run out	28
J Edrich	c Engineer b Abid Ali	0	b Bedi	59
K Fletcher	lbw b Abid Ali	1	not out	28
B D'Oliveira	c Gavaskar b Abid Ali	12	not out	23
A Knott†	b Venkataraghavan	41		
R Illingworth(c)	c Gavaskar b Venkataraghavan	107		
R Hutton	c & b Venkataraghavan	15		
P Lever	not out	88		
N Gifford	c Engineer b Solkar	8		
J Price	run out	0		
Extras	(b 6, lb 12, nb 2, w 1)	21	(lb 5, nb 1)	6
Team score		386		245/3d

Fall of wickets 1st innings: 1-21, 2-21, 3-25, 4-41, 5-116, 6-168, 7-187, 8-355, 9-384, 10-386

Fall of wickets 2nd innings: 1-44, 2-167, 3-212

Bowling figures	O	M	R	W	O	M	R	W
S Abid Ali	32.4	5	64	4	26	2	95	0
E Solkar	21	5	46	1	5	0	23	1
B Chandrasekhar	30	6	90	0	2	0	5	0
B Bedi	40	10	72	1	5	0	21	1
S Venkataraghavan	35	9	89	3	16	3	58	0
S Gavaskar	2	0	4	0	12	3	37	0

INDIA	FIRST INNINGS		SECOND INNINGS	
A Mankad	c Knott b Lever	8	b Price	7
S Gavaskar	c Knott b Price	57	c Knott b Hutton	24
A Wadekar (c)	c Knott b Hutton	12	b Price	9
D Sardesai	b Lever	14	not out	13
G Viswanath	b Lever	10	not out	8
F Engineer†	c Edrich b Lever	22		
E Solkar	c Hutton b D'Oliveira	50		
S Abid Ali	b D'Oliveira	0		
S Venkataraghavan	c Knott b Lever	20		
B Bedi	b Price	8		
B Chandrasekhar	not out	4		
Extras	(b 1, lb 4, nb 2)	7	(lb 2, nb 2)	4
Team score		212		65/3

Fall of wickets 1st innings: 1-19, 2-52, 3-90, 4-103, 5-104, 6-163, 7-164, 8-194, 9-200, 10-212

Fall of wickets 2nd innings: 1-9, 2-22, 3-50

Bowling figures	O	M	R	W	O	M	R	W
J Price	22	7	44	2	10	3	30	2
P Lever	26	4	70	5	7	3	14	0
B D'Oliveira	24	11	40	2	3	2	1	0
R Hutton	14	3	35	1	7	1	16	1
R Illingworth	7	2	16	0				

Ray Illingworth led a formidable England side that had triumphed in Australia earlier in 1970-71.

Syed Kirmani Sleeps in the Dressing Room

The 21-year-old Syed Kirmani featured in only seven out of the 16 tour matches India played in England in 1971. With Farokh Engineer 'keeping in the Tests and P Krishnamurthy doing the honours for majority of the other games, Kirmani was largely on the bench.

Sunil Gavaskar narrated a funny incident from that tour which involves Kirmani. The young wicketkeeper loved to take his afternoon naps, even during games. RP Mehra, the noted administrator, was on tour and woke up Kirmani during one of the matches against Kent, asking him to observe and learn from the wicketkeeper Alan Knott.

Kirmani obliged until Mehra left the dressing room for a smoke. The gloveman quickly made his way to the physio's room and went into slumber. On his return to the dressing room, Mehra asked about Kirmani and was told that he was watching Knott from the sightscreen. A happy Mehra went on to say that all youngsters need is a push at times blissfully unaware that Kirmani was fast asleep[100].

---

100 Sunil Gavaskar, Idols. Chapter – Syed Kirmani. Published by Rupa and Co 1983 Fourth Impression. P. 265.

On the tour to England, he scored 118 runs in nine innings at an average of 23.60, with seven catches behind the stumps. About five years later, Kirmani made his debut for India post Engineer's retirement. That he went on to become one of India's greatest wicketkeepers is proof of the selector's foresight in picking him in 1971. In a decade-long career, Kirmani went on to play 88 Tests and was also a critical part of India's 1983 World Cup winning side.

A promising wicketkeeper in 1971, **Syed Kirmani** was picked to tour England. However, he had to wait until 1976 to don the international cap for India. He remains one of the best wicketkeepers India has produced.

Yorkshire vs Indians – India tour of England 1971 - Tour Match

Dates: 11-13 August 1971 (3-day First-Class match)
Venue: Headingley, Leeds
Toss: Unknown
Scores: Indians 145, Yorkshire 137/3
Result: Draw

INDIANS	FIRST INNINGS	
A Ali Baig	b Cooper	28
K Jayantilal	c Old b Hutton	14
A Wadekar(c)	c Sharpe b Hutton	59
D Sardesai	b Cooper	1
G Viswanath	c Smith b Wilson	10
E Solkar	b Old	17
S Venkataraghavan	c Lumb b Wilson	2
D Govindraj	c Cooper b Wilson	5
P Krishnamurthy†	not out	2
E Prasanna	b Old	0
B Bedi	c Cooper b Old	2
Extras	(lb 3, nb 2)	5
Team score		145

Fall of wickets 1-34, 2-68, 3-89, 4-112, 5-127, 6-133, 7-141, 8-141, 9-141, 10-145

Bowling figures	O	M	R	W
C Old	15	5	33	3
R Hutton	12	5	28	2
H Cooper	12	5	36	2
G Cope	13	5	31	0
D Wilson	11	6	12	3

YORKSHIRE	FIRST INNINGS	
B Leadbeater	c Jayantilal b Venkataraghavan	40
R Lumb	not out	57
J Hampshire	c Viswanath b Prasanna	10
A Dalton	c Venkataraghavan b Bedi	7
R Hutton	not out	9
Extras	(b 9, lb 4, w 1)	14
Team score		137/3

Did not bat – N Smith†, P Sharpe, D Wilson(c), C Old, G Cope, H Cooper

Fall of wickets 1-76, 2-91, 3-119

Bowling figures	O	M	R	W
D Govindraj	14	3	39	0
E Solkar	8	4	8	0
E Prasanna	12	2	24	1
B Bedi	17	9	28	1
S Venkataraghavan	10	3	24	1

Chandrasekhar Seals His Spot with a Six-For against Nottinghamshire

Bhagwat Chandrasekhar had arrived in England with the pressure to perform to retain his status as a Test cricketer. Making a comeback to the Test side, Chandrasekhar was given an ultimatum to perform by the chairman of selectors, Vijay Merchant. He started the tour well with a five-wicket haul in the first game against Middlesex and continued the good form with a tally of 11 scalps against Leicestershire. In the first Test at Lord's, he picked a total of five wickets. However, the leg-spinner felt the pressure after he went wicketless at Old Trafford in the second Test.

"Before this Test (third at The Oval) there was speculation that I might be the bowler to be left out," Chandrasekhar said[101]. He was eventually picked for the third Test. He believed it was because the manager Col Hemu Adhikari "settled the matter" and Wadekar also showed belief.

However, Wadekar had made up his mind about his spot after Chandrasekhar's performance in the tour game against Nottinghamshire just before the third Test. There was a toss-up

---

101 Rajan Bala, The Winning Hand, Biography of BS Chandrasekhar. Published by Rupa and Co 1993, p. 53

between Chandrasekhar and Erapalli Prasanna but the former responded with a spell of six for 34 on the final day to rattle Nottinghamshire. "There could be no doubts about his place at the Oval," Wadekar said[102].

Thus Chandrasekhar retained his spot and created history at The Oval. His Karnataka teammate, Prasanna, did not get a Test on the tour.

---

102 My Cricketing Years, Ajit Wadekar as told to KN Prabhu, p. 114. Published by Vikas Publishing House Pvt Ltd 1973

Nottinghamshire vs Indians – India tour of England 1971 – Tour Match

Dates: 14-17 August 1971 (3-day First-Class rest day on 15 August)
Venue: Trent Bridge, Nottingham
Toss: Unknown
Scores: Indians 168/6d & 145/4d, Nottinghamshire 69/7d & 115/6
Result: Draw

INDIA	FIRST INNINGS		SECOND INNINGS	
S Gavaskar	c Smedley b W Taylor	7	c Pullan b W Taylor	8
A Mankad	c Hassan b White	22	not out	50
A Wadekar(c)	b M Taylor	49	c Hassan b M Taylor	26
D Sardesai	not out	57	c Frost b Plummer	19
G Viswanath	hit wicket b M Taylor	12	b White	38
E Solkar	run out	2		
S Abid Ali	run out	2		
D Govindraj	not out	4		
Extras	(lb 11, nb 2)	13	(lb 3, nb 1)	4
Team score		168/6d		145/4d

Did not bat – S Kirmani†, E Prasanna, B Chandrasekhar

Fall of wickets 1st innings: 1-14, 2-71, 3-93, 4-138, 5-142, 6-154

Fall of wickets 2nd innings: 1-13, 2-51, 3-80, 4-145

Bowling figures	O	M	R	W	O	M	R	W
B Stead	11	2	18	0	9	0	37	0
W Taylor	15	3	33	1	7	0	30	1
B White	18	7	42	1	4.3	0	20	1
M Taylor	17	4	44	2	8	1	30	1
P Plummer	7	2	18	0	6	1	24	1

NOTTINGHAMSHIRE	FIRST INNINGS		SECOND INNINGS	
G Frost	lbw b Abid Ali	14	c & b Chandrasekhar	50
B White	run out	5	c Solkar b Chandrasekhar	2
M Smedley	c Kirmani b Abid Ali	2	b Chandrasekhar	0
B Bolus(c)	lbw b Abid Ali	16	lbw b Chandrasekhar	30
R Bielby	b Govindraj	0	c sub b Chandrasekhar	1
B Hassan	c Kirmani b Govindraj	0	b Chandrasekhar	9
M Taylor	not out	19	not out	9
P Plummer	b Chandrasekhar	11	not out	6
D Pullan†	not out	0		
Extras	(lb 2)	2	(b 6, lb 2)	8
Team score		69/7d		115/6

Did not bat – B Stead, W Taylor

Fall of wickets 1st innings: 1-7, 2-22, 3-23, 4-36, 5-36, 6-40, 7-63

Fall of wickets 2nd innings: 1-56, 2-60, 3-80, 4-95, 5-97, 6-100

Bowling figures	O	M	R	W	O	M	R	W
D Govindraj	11	2	37	2	6	1	23	0
S Abid Ali	13.3	6	23	3	7	0	30	0
B Chandrasekhar	3	0	7	1	20	8	34	6
E Prasanna					18	10	18	0
E Solkar					1	0	2	0

Ashok Mankad Greets
John Snow

Ashok Mankad opened the batting with Sunil Gavaskar in all the Tests in England but failed to make a major impact. What helped Mankad retain his spot at the top was that he scored runs in the tour matches with the other options such as Abbas Ali Baig and Kenia Jayantilal failing to find consistency. In the three Tests, he accounted for only 42 runs, with the highest of 11 coming during India's successful run-chase in the third and final Test at The Oval. However, his overall First-Class stats on the tour were impressive with 795 runs in 13 matches at an average of 41.84 which included two centuries and four fifties.

Ajit Wadekar recalled Mankad maintaining his sense of humour through the tour despite the torrid time in Tests. Through the tour, Mankad would greet England's most fearsome fast bowler, John Snow, by saying, "Good morning, sir. I'm Ashok Mankad. I hope I'll get runs against you.[103]" Snow had made quite an impression in Australia and was England's trump card. Mankad though was unfazed by his threat or his own tough run.

In fact, at the end of the Tests, he even joked about his own poor returns, leaving his teammates in splits. This was just after he

---

103 'Good morning, sir. I hope I'll get runs against you', Cricinfo. Published on August 1, 2008. Accessed at: https://www.espncricinfo.com/story/good-morning-sir-i-hope-i-ll-get-runs-against-you-363215

recorded his highest score of the Test series in the last innings – which was 11. "A pity the Tests are over. I was just getting into my stride and by the fifth Test I would have surely scored 25 runs," he remarked after being dismissed at The Oval[104].

Mankad did not play the home series against England the following year. He made a comeback to the Indian team on the ill-fated tour to England in 1974 and played his last Test match on the tour to Australia in 1977-78.

104 Sunil Gavaskar, Sunny Days – Sunil Gavaskar's Own Story p 66, Published by Rupa and Co. Nineteenth Impression 2005

Ashok Mankad had a tough time in the Tests in England but was very
consistent in the First-Class matches on tour.

The Mill Reef

John Edrich walked out to bat at No. 3 on Day Four of the third Test at The Oval with England 94 ahead in the second essay. John Jameson had just been the first wicket to fall, with Bhagwat Chandrasekhar getting a touch onto a ball hit back at him, which then shattered the stumps at the non-striker's end. Fortune had smiled on the Indians and Chandrasekhar was to be its pall-bearer through the rest of the day. Edrich, a solid left-hander, was an important scalp.

Chandrasekhar plotted Edrich's downfall in his mind. However, Dilip Sardesai called out to him and said, "Mill Reef Daalo." (Hindi for: Bowl a Mill Reef). On that tour, Chandrasekhar and Sardesai keenly followed the horse races and one contender had particularly caught their eye. Named Mill Reef, the American-bred horse, was the toast of the races in 1971 and was also the champion of the famous Derby.

"Half-way through in to the run-up, I changed my grip and bowled the faster one," said Chandrasekhar[105]. He unleashed a faster one that castled the solid defence of Edrich to give India their second wicket.

The Karnataka leggie had his first wicket of the innings and five more were to follow as he setup India's historic maiden win on

---

105 Aditya Bhushan and Sachin Bajaj, Fortune Turners: The Quartet that spun India to glory, p. 97-98. Published by Global Cricket School - 2019

English soil. A man who wasn't considered for the tour to the West Indies and wasn't confident of playing at The Oval went on to become the ultimate match-winner on tour. England were bowled out for 101 and Chandrasekhar ended with figures of six for 38. India were left with a target of 173.

'The Winning Hand'... **Bhagwat Chandrasekhar**'s six-wicket haul at The Oval is a part of Indian cricket folklore as it inspired the team to record its first Test win on English soil.

Knott's Missing Bails

Alan Knott had troubled the Indian bowlers through the series with the bat. In the first innings at The Oval, he scored 90 to take England past 300. With BS Chandrasekhar wreaking havoc, Knott walked in at 49 for four with the task of steadying the innings. The street-smart Eknath Solkar thought of an unorthodox plan to unsettle Knott even before he took strike. The English wicket-keeper batsman would mark his guard using his bail, a style made famous in modern times by Shivnarine Chanderpaul.

Solkar asked skipper Ajit Wadekar if he could take the bails off before Knott marks his guard and if it was within the laws. Wadekar told him it wasn't against the law but asked the all-rounder to put the bails back on before the ball is bowled[106]. "I have noticed that whenever Knott takes his guard, he has a habit of marking it with a bail. I just want to see if not having a bail would affect him psychologically," said Solkar[107]. Knott was forced to abandon his practice as he couldn't find the bail on the stump and instead marked his guard with his shoe. Did that disturb Knott? A few balls later, Solkar had an even bigger role to play in Knott's downfall.

---

106 Mihir Bose, The Nine Waves – The Extraordinary Story of Indian Cricket. Published by Aleph Book Company 2019. Chapter: Surprise.

107 When Ajit Wadekar Reminisced The Summer of '71. BCCI Official Website. Published on August 16, 2018. Accessed at: https://www.bcci.tv/articles/2018/news/99893/when-ajit-wadekar-reminisced-the-summer-of-71

Earlier in the innings, Solkar had taken a great catch to dismiss Keith Fletcher at his customary spot at forward short-leg. Knowing the importance of Knott's wicket, Solkar was all the more alert for not only half a chance but as he said "even the quarter-chance".[108] S Venkataraghavan soon found the edge off Knott's bat and onto his pad. "I went into the dive of my life and somehow got there! For an agonising moment the ball rested on the finger-tips of my 'cupped' hands and could have dropped off," Solkar said[109]. Solkar managed to hold on to what many describe as his best catch ever. Knott was done in for a solitary run by the Solkar magic.

Solkar is still considered India's greatest fielder at short-leg, whose flashing reflexes had the batsmen on their toes while facing the Indian spinners. Across the two tours, he accounted for 14 catches in the Tests – six of which came during the victory at Trinidad and two during England's collapse at The Oval.

108 Eknath Solkar, My Best Catches, The Illustrated Weekly of India, Vol C, June 10-16, 1979, p. 35
109 Ibid

Bella the Elephant

Having delayed their departure to England by two days on the advice of an astrologer, the Indians were known to look out for good omen. When they resumed their nervy run-chase of 173 on the final day at The Oval, they couldn't have had a better omen to affirm a happy ending. Bella, a baby elephant from Chessington Zoo, was brought to The Oval by a few passionate Indian fans. What made it symbolic was the fact that August 24, 1971 was Ganesh Chaturthi – a very auspicious day in the Hindu calendar, which celebrates Ganesha – the elephant-headed deity. In captain Ajit Wadekar's home state of Maharashtra, this is possibly the biggest festival after Diwali.

India's start to the day was shaky as Wadekar was run out for 45 very early. As Wadekar walked back at 76 for three, his inner Maharashtrian looked up at the skies and prayed, "As I came back to the pavillion I prayed to Lord Ganesha, imploring him to make the victory possible, having raised our hopes with his appearance that morning. The rest is history.[110]"

Bella walked on the outfield as the runs ticked over and India approached the win. It was as if divine forces had come together to bless India. The rain at Lord's and Manchester

---

110 Simon Burnton, A first win in England: India and the elephant will never forget. The Guardian. Published on August 21, 2018. Accessed at: https://www.theguardian.com/sport/2018/aug/21/first-win-england-india-elephant-never-forget

were signs and this was confirmation that it was India's time to shine.

Incidentally, Bella was only purchased by Chessington Zoo the previous year from a pet shop in Birmingham called Tyseley Pet Stores.

Abid Ali Hits the Winning Runs

Following the early dismissal of Ajit Wadekar on Day Five at The Oval, Gundappa Viswanath and Dilip Sardesai stabilised the Indian run-chase. Both batsmen took all the time in the world as the target wasn't very imposing but the weight of potential history added the pressure. Sardesai faced 156 balls for his 40 before being dismissed by Derek Underwood. Soon after, India lost Eknath Solkar. At 134 for five, they were still 39 runs away from a victory. In walked Farokh Engineer and decided to absorb the pressure with a cautious approach. "I was determined not to play a single loose shot. In fact, throughout the match, I had been uncharacteristically careful," Engineer described his approach[111]. Engineer had scored a boundary-less fifty in the first innings and brought in the same grit during those nervy times. This from a man who once scored 94 runs before lunch on Day One!

With India on the cusp of victory, Viswanath's 171-ball vigil for 33 ended when Brian Luckhurst had him caught behind. S Abid Ali, the man who batted with Sunil Gavaskar during the victorious moments at Trinidad earlier in the year, walked in for a second shot at history. "I told him not to do anything silly because there were only Bishen and Chandra to follow and neither knew which end of the bat to hold!" remarked Engineer[112]. One must note that

---

111 Farokh Engineer, 'Keep the change, Outlook Cricket Special: 75 Years of Indian Cricket p. 64, 2004
112 Ibid

S Venkataraghavan was in the hut too – who was more than capable with the bat.

"I should thank Farokh (Engineer) for telling me not to worry as to who should finish off the match. If you get a chance just complete the formality," is Abid's version of the story[113]. Soon after, he cut one through the off-side and the crowd invaded the field even before the ball could get to the boundary. Mere formality, considering the writing was on the wall.

Many Indians flocked onto the field and Abid was lifted on shoulders – bringing memories of the scenes from Trinidad when India sealed the series. Engineer said, "India was a colony of England, and to beat your masters at their own game was a bit of a feather in the cap. Any victory in a Test series was joyous, but to beat England in England was a phenomenal feat at the time for us Indians.[114]"

As the dust settled, captain Wadekar and his players came out onto the balcony to wave to all their legion of supporters. For a country that was only 24 years old and finding its feet in the international arena in every sphere, this was in a sense an announcement of India's presence. That it coincided with an epochal time in the geopolitical area made it all the more special. Sporting achievements are often expressions of a country's society! The cricketing success that year mirrored India's growing confidence in itself as an independent nation.

---

113 VV Subrahmanyam, 'It was a huge honour for me', The Hindu. Published on July 20, 2011. Accessed at: https://www.thehindu.com/sport/cricket/it-was-a-huge-honour-for-me/article2260485.ece

114 Engineer told *The Times. Sourced from: https://www.espncricinfo.com/story/rewind-to-1971-india-s-day-of-glory-527248*

Hatteea Watches India Win at the Oval

"I had tears in my eyes and was absolutely overwhelmed," says former Bombay player Saeed Ahmed Hatteea, who was at The Oval when Abid Ali hit the winning runs. "I was not in the changing room but in the stands. For me, I felt as if I was part of the team and it was my country that had beaten England on English soil," he said looking back at that historic day. Although, things could have been very different and Hatteea could well have been a part of the Indian dressing room that year.

In *Sunny Days*, Sunil Gavaskar writes about sharing a train-ride with Hatteea on the day the team was to be announced, with both men hoping for selection. While Gavaskar was picked, Hatteea missed out.

Hatteea said, "Deep down inside my heart there was something that said maybe I should have been in that changing room – maybe I should have been in the balcony with them. But it wasn't – that was it." A fast bowler, Hatteea had lived a major part of his life in England but had come down to play for Bombay, making a mark for them in the 1969-70 season. In the Duleep Trophy, held ahead of the selection in 1971, he had made quite an impression by dismissing Mansur Ali Khan Pataudi.

However, the selectors picked only D Govindraj as the fast bowler with the all-rounders S Abid Ali and Eknath Solkar sharing the new ball duties. "Whilst I was very sad and disappointed at not being selected to go to the West Indies, I am not in any way critical of anyone. I respect the job selectors have and the difficulty they had in selecting the side," Hatteea said.

Interestingly, Hatteea's first son was born during India's tour to England. Since the players weren't paid well, with a family to look after, Hatteea stayed back in England and focused on his job. He said, "When I came back to England, I had little choice but to start working. In those days you had to be employed by Mafatlal, ACC or a large corporation or you had to be a part of a royal family and I was neither. I started working and once I did my career and work took over.[115]"

---

115 Conversation with the author

Ajit Wadekar Takes a Nap in the Dressing Room in Tense Run-Chase

Dilip Sardesai played one through the off-side and called his captain Ajit Wadekar for a quick single. The southpaw scampered across but Basil D'Oliveira's accurate throw found him short. A dejected Wadekar had to walk back to the pavillion, failing to add to his overnight tally of 45. India were still 97 short of victory, with seven wickets in hand on a nervy final day at The Oval. The captain had set the tone for the series at Lord's with an attacking innings of 85 and wanted to seal this historic opportunity with a calming knock.

In partnership with Sardesai, Gundappa Viswanath stabilised the innings but the runs weren't easy to score. In the dressing room, Wadekar decided to take a nap and relax. "You know we were so sure of victory and the atmosphere in the dressing room was so relaxed that after chatting to (S) Venkataraghavan and (Farokh) Engineer, I settled into a chair and couldn't help falling asleep," Wadekar said[116].

---

116 Ashish Magotra, 'While I was Sleeping'. Mumbai Mirror. Published on August 15, 2007. Accessed at: https://mumbaimirror.indiatimes.com/sport/cricket/while-i-was-sleeping/articleshow/15732620.cms

Wadekar may have missed out on watching the pinnacle of his captaincy unfold in the middle but was ready to soak in all the deserving accolades coming his way. On India's victory, Ken Barrington, the great England batsman who was then their manager, came to wake Wadekar up and tell him of his duties as winning captain.

England vs India – 3rd Test – India tour of England 1971

Dates: 19-24 August 1971 (5-day Test match with rest day on 22 Aug)
Venue: The Oval, London
Toss: England, chose to bat
Scores: ENG 355 & 101, IND 284 & 174/6
Result: India won by 4 wickets
Series status: India won the series 1-0

ENGLAND	FIRST INNINGS		SECOND INNINGS	
B Luckhurst	c Gavaskar b Solkar	1	c Venkataraghavan b Chandrasekhar	33
J Jameson	run out	82	run out (Chandrasekhar)	16
J Edrich	c Engineer b Bedi	41	b Chandrasekhar	0
K Fletcher	c Gavaskar b Bedi	1	c Solkar b Chandrasekhar	0
B D'Oliveira	c Mankad b Chandrasekhar	2	c sub b Venkataraghavan	17
A Knott†	c & b Solkar	90	c Solkar b Venkataraghavan	1
R Illingworth(c)	b Chandrasekhar	11	c & b Chandrasekhar	4
R Hutton	b Venkataraghavan	81	not out	13
J Snow	c Engineer b Solkar	3	c & b Chandrasekhar	0
D Underwood	c Wadekar b Venkataraghavan	22	c Mankad b Bedi	11
J Price	not out	1	lbw b Chandrasekhar	3
Extras	(b 4, lb 15, w 1)	20	(lb 3)	3
Team score		355		101

Fall of wickets 1st innings: 1-5, 2-111, 3-135, 4-139, 5-143, 6-175, 7-278, 8-284, 9-352, 10-355

Fall of wickets 2nd innings: 1-23, 2-24, 3-24, 4-49, 5-54, 6-65, 7-72, 8-72, 9-96, 10-101

Bowling figures	O	M	R	W	O	M	R	W
S Abid Ali	12	2	47	0	3	1	5	0
E Solkar	15	4	28	3	3	1	10	0
S Gavaskar	1	0	1	0				
B Bedi	36	5	120	2	1	0	1	1
B Chandrasekhar	24	6	76	2	18.1	3	38	6
S Venkataraghavan	20.4	3	63	2	20	4	44	2

INDIA	FIRST INNINGS		SECOND INNINGS	
S Gavaskar	b Snow	6	lbw b Snow	0
A Mankad	b Price	10	c Hutton b Underwood	11
A Wadekar(c)	b Illingworth	48	run out	45
D Sardesai	b Illingworth	54	c Knott b Underwood	40
G Viswanath	b Illingworth	0	c Knott b Luckhurst	33
E Solkar	c Fletcher b D'Oliveira	44	c & b Underwood	1
F Engineer	c Illingworth b Snow	59	not out	28
S Abid Ali	b Illingworth	26	not out	4
S Venkataraghavan	lbw b Underwood	24		
B Bedi	c D'Oliveira b Illingworth	2		
B Chandrasekhar	not out	0		
Extras	(b 6, lb 4, nb 1)	11	(b 6, lb 5, nb 1)	12
Team score		284		174/6

Fall of wickets 1st innings: 1-17, 2-21, 3-114, 4-118, 5-125, 6-222, 7-230, 8-278, 9-284, 10-284

Fall of wickets 2nd innings: 1-2, 2-37, 3-76, 4-124, 5-134, 6-170

Bowling figures	O	M	R	W	O	M	R	W
J Snow	24	5	68	2	11	7	14	1
J Price	15	2	51	1	5	0	10	0
R Hutton	12	2	30	0				
B D'Oliveira	7	5	5	1	9	3	17	0
R Illingworth	34.3	12	70	5	36	15	40	0
D Underwood	25	6	49	1	38	14	72	3
B Luckhurst					2	0	9	1

Gavaskar Curry, Chandrasekhar Soup Et Al

The euphoria of the Indian win at The Oval was unparalleled. Up until then, it was arguably India's finest moment in the sport. The outpour of emotion and celebration at The Oval reflected the magnitude of the event. For a country that was ruled by the United Kingdom for many years, sporting success against them, that too in their own backyard, was a momentous occasion. Not only was it huge for the millions back home in India but also those who had settled in the UK and were earning their bread.

Although India were slated to play a First-Class game the day after the third and final Test, the players did manage to let their hair down. The disciplinarian, Col Hemu Adhikari, did not enforce his usual regimes and let the team soak in the moment. The team celebrated the occasion at an Indian restaurant, which had hilariously rebranded its menu to include items such as Gavaskar Curry, Wadekar Cutlet, Chandrasekhar Soup and Bedi Pulao[117].

Following the celebrations, India made it to Brighton late in the night and took the field to face Sussex the next day. Farokh Engineer drove down to Manchester to turn up for Lancashire against Derbyshire.

---

117 My Cricketing Years, Ajit Wadekar as told to KN Prabhu, p. 119. Published by Vikas Publishing House Pvt Ltd 1973

The next morning, Sunil Gavaskar and Kenia Jayantilal walked out to open the batting against Sussex. Eknath Solkar's 90 helped take India to 220. In reply, Sussex got 386. The three-day encounter was a drawn affair. The tour continued for India though as the day after they finished their tour game against Sussex, they took on Somerset at Taunton. Solkar and S Abid Ali's centuries were the highlights of that match for the tourists.

India did get a day's break after the Somerset game before taking on Worcertershire at New Road. The tour ended with a final First-Class match against the TN Pearce's XI. While the Tests were the major focus, the tour games formed an integral part of the visit to England.

Sussex vs Indians – India tour of England 1971 – Tour Match
Dates: 25-27 Aug 1971 (3-day First-Class match)
Venue: County Ground, Hove
Toss: Unknown
Scores: Indians 220, 276/7 & Sussex 386/9d
Result: Draw

INDIANS	FIRST INNINGS		SECOND INNINGS	
S Gavaskar	c Parks b Greig	37	b Joshi	40
K Jayantilal	lbw b Spencer	15	c Parks b Joshi	57
A Ali Baig	c Joshi b Spencer	13	c Greig b Graves	4
E Solkar	c Joshi b Greig	90	c Greig b Joshi	6
G Viswanath	b Greig	24	c Graves b Buss	38
A Wadekar(c)	run out	3	st Parks b Joshi	25
S Abid Ali	b Greig	11	b Joshi	13
S Kirmani†	c Snow b Joshi	16	not out	37
D Govindraj	lbw b Buss	1	not out	40
E Prasanna	b Buss	1		
B Bedi	not out	3		
Extras	(lb 4, nb 2)	6	(b 4, lb 3, nb 7, w 2)	16
Team score		220		276/7

Fall of wickets 1st innings: 1-45, 2-64, 3-69, 4-105, 5-110, 6-126, 7-197, 8-202, 9-208, 10-220

Fall of wickets 2nd innings: 1-66, 2-80, 3-91, 4-132, 5-181, 6-195, 7-195

Bowling figures	O	M	R	W	O	M	R	W
J Snow	13	2	39	0	11	3	33	0
T Greig	25.3	3	78	4	20	6	47	0
M Buss	23	12	30	2	11	5	18	1
J Spencer	15	2	34	2	6	3	12	0
J Denman	3	1	13	0	3	0	20	0
U Joshi	10	1	20	1	51	16	107	5
P Graves					26	19	23	1

SUSSEX	FIRST INNINGS	
M Buss	c Bedi	140
G Greenidge	c Govindraj b Prasanna	62
R Prideaux	b Prasanna	39
J Parks†	lbw b Prasanna	15
T Greig	c Kirmani b Bedi	11
P Graves	c Jayantilal b Prasanna	34
M Griffith(c)	b Prasanna	14
J Snow	c & b Bedi	23
J Denman	b Solkar	9
J Spencer	not out	18
U Joshi	not out	0
Extras	(b 5, lb 13, nb 1, w 2)	21
Team score		386/9d

Fall of wickets 1-199, 2-213, 3-248, 4-277, 5-299, 6-318, 7-330, 8-366, 9-366

Bowling figures	O	M	R	W
D Govindraj	10	2	40	0
S Abid Ali	19	3	65	0
E Solkar	6	0	18	1
B Bedi	44	14	105	3
E Prasanna	43	6	137	5

Somerset vs Indians – India tour of England 1971 – Tour Match

Dates: 28-30 August 1971 (3-day First-Class match)
Venue: County Ground, Taunton
Toss: Indians, chose to bat
Scores: Indians 349/8d & 162/5d, Somerset 226/4d & 127/2
Result: Draw

INDIANS	FIRST INNINGS		SECOND INNINGS	
K Jayantilal	c Virgin b Cartwright	32	c Taylor b Jones	2
A Mankad	b Cartwright	26	b O'Keeffe	21
A Wadekar(c)	b Cartwright	10	c Virgin b Cartwright	74
D Sardesai	b Cartwright	9	b Cartwright	6
A Ali Baig	c Moseley b Cartwright	24	c Langford b Cartwright	20
E Solkar	c Langford b O'Keeffe	113		
S Abid Ali	not out	102	not out	17
S Venkataraghavan	c Clarkson b Jones	4	not out	15
P Krishnamurthy†	b O'Keeffe	7		
D Govindraj	not out	10		
Extras	(b 4, lb 1, nb 6, w 1)	12	(b 4, lb 1, nb 2)	7
Team score		349/8d		162/5d

Fall of wickets 1st innings: 1-57, 2-72, 3-73, 4-87, 5-158, 6-292, 7-299, 8-320

Fall of wickets 2nd innings: 1-7, 2-58, 3-67, 4-128, 5-130

Bowling figures	O	M	R	W	O	M	R	W
A Jones	17	0	83	1	7	1	32	1
H Moseley	14	1	58	0	5	0	11	0
T Cartwright	33	13	79	5	15	5	42	3
K O'Keeffe	24.4	8	76	2	8	2	20	1
B Langford	11	1	41	0	7	1	40	0
R Virgin					1	0	10	0

SOMERSET	FIRST INNINGS		SECOND INNINGS	
R Virgin	c Wadekar b Venkataraghavan	47	c Mankad b Govindraj	0
M Kitchen	c Wadekar b Abid Ali	5	c Abid Ali b Venkataraghavan	27
B Close	not out	103	not out	43
T Clarkson	lbw b Chandrasekhar	4		
K O'Keeffe	run out	35		
P Robinson	not out	13	not out	52
Extras	(lb 15, nb 4)	19	(b 2, lb 3)	5
Team score		226/4d		127/2

Did not bat – T Cartwright, D Taylor†, H Moseley, B Langford(c), A Jones

Fall of wickets 1st innings: 1-40, 2-94, 3-123, 4-194

Fall of wickets 2nd innings: 1-0, 2-50

Bowling figures	O	M	R	W	O	M	R	W
D Govindraj	10	1	32	0	6	0	24	1
S Abid Ali	17	3	42	1	3	1	3	0
E Solkar	11	2	28	0				
B Chandrasekhar	16.3	7	38	1	11	2	31	0
S Venkataraghavan	25	6	67	1	12	2	43	1
A Wadekar					4	1	16	0
A Mankad					3	1	5	0

Worcestershire vs Indians – India tour of England 1971 – Tour Match

Dates: 1-3 September 1971 (3-day First-Class match)
Venue: County Ground, New Road, Worcester
Toss: Unknown
Scores: Indians 383/3d & 150/8d, Worcestershire 248 & 250/5
Result: Draw

INDIANS	FIRST INNINGS		SECOND INNINGS	
K Jayantilal	b Carter	2	c Parker b Carter	4
S Gavaskar	c Yardley b Wilkinson	194	c Headley b Carter	6
A Wadekar(c)	c Parker b Wilkinson	150		
G Viswanath	not out	22	c Yardley b Wilkinson	53
D Sardesai	not out	0	st Wilcock b Griffith	13
E Solkar			c sub b Wilkinson	14
S Abid Ali			c Carter b Griffith	23
S Venkataraghavan			b Wilkinson	12
S Kirmani†			not out	3
B Bedi			c Stimpson b Griffith	7
B Chandrasekhar			not out	4
Extras	(b 1, lb 6, nb 8)	15	(lb 6, nb 3, w 2)	11
Team score		383/3d		150/8d

Fall of wickets 1st innings: 1-2, 2-329, 3-373

Fall of wickets 2nd innings: 1-9, 2-14, 3-40, 4-57, 5-106, 6-121, 7-134, 8-145

Bowling figures	O	M	R	W	O	M	R	W
V Holder	18	2	64	0				
R Carter	23	2	81	1	8	1	18	2
K Wilkinson	30	6	84	2	17	3	48	3
I Khan	16	0	73	0	5	1	15	0
K Griffith	25	5	66	0	14	3	58	3

WORCESTERSHIRE	FIRST INNINGS		SECOND INNINGS	
R Headley(c)	c Venkataraghavan b Chandrasekhar	25	c & b Solkar	13
P Stimpson	lbw b Bedi	24	c Wadekar b Abid Ali	5
A Ormrod	c Chandrasekhar b Bedi	16	b Abid Ali	76
J Yardley	b Venkataraghavan	18	not out	104
J Parker	c Gavaskar b Abid Ali	91		
I Khan	run out	0	b Abid Ali	15
K Wilkinson	c Solkar b Venkataraghavan	48		
K Griffith	b Venkataraghavan	1		
G Wilcock†	b Venkataraghavan	0		
V Holder	c Abid Ali b Solkar	9	b Solkar	27
R Carter	not out	0		
Extras	(b 8, lb 5, nb 3)	16	(b 3, lb 6, nb 1)	10
Team score		248		250/5

Fall of wickets 1st innings: 1-53, 2-53, 3-90, 4-92, 5-92, 6-192, 7-208, 8-208, 9-246, 10-248

Fall of wickets 2nd innings: 1-18, 2-26, 3-165, 4-202, 5-250

Bowling figures	O	M	R	W	O	M	R	W
S Abid Ali	7.4	1	26	1	21	2	64	3
E Solkar	10	2	24	1	20.5	2	85	2
B Bedi	27	9	50	2	10	0	41	0
S Venkataraghavan	34	11	60	4	9	1	31	0
B Chandrasekhar	27	8	66	1	3	0	19	0
S Gavaskar	2	1	6	0				

'Only Hindi' Says
Wadekar to Johnston

Brian Johnston was one of the well-known cricket commentators on the BBC. During India's tour to England in 1971, he had developed a rapport with the visiting captain Ajit Wadekar. During one of the matches, the Indian captain decided to pull a prank on his English friend, leaving the veteran broadcaster stumped and baffled.

As was the practice, Johnston was tasked with the responsibility of interviewing batsmen soon after they were dismissed. Wadekar walked back after he was out and Johnston approached him for a quick chat near the boundary.

"No English," Wadekar proclaimed to Johnston's surprise. The commentator pursued Wadekar and kept asking him questions even as the latter said, "No English."

A baffled Johnston then said, "Ajit, you have been talking to me throughout this tour in English. How could you forget English so soon?" The Indian captain didn't relent in his prank and then said, "Only Hindi!"

Talk about a language barrier[118]!

---

118 Clayton Murzello and Sandeep Patil, Caught and Told, Published by Roli Books 2007. p. 110

TN Pearce's XI vs Indians – India tour of England 1971 – Tour Match

Dates: 4-7 September 1971 (3-day First-Class match with rest day on 5 September)
Venue: North Marine Road, Scarborough
Toss: Unknown
Scores: TN Pearce's XI 357/3d & 199/3d, Indians 306 & 252/5
Result: Indians won by 5 wickets

TN PEARCE'S XI	FIRST INNINGS		SECOND INNINGS	
R Virgin	st Krishnamurthy b Solkar	176	lbw b Chandrasekhar	22
B Bolus	run out	75	not out	106
P Parfitt	c Mankad b Chandrasekhar	4	b Bedi	63
K Fletcher	not out	67		
T Lewis(c)	not out	21	not out	1
B Close	c Govindraj b Bedi	1		
Extras	(b 12, lb 1, w 1)	14	(b 6)	6
Team score		357/3d		199/3d

Did not bat – B Taylor†, P Walker, R Hobbs, K Boyce, J Price

Fall of wickets 1st innings: 1-155, 2-164, 3-308

Fall of wickets 2nd innings: 1-47, 2-190, 3-194

Bowling figures	O	M	R	W	O	M	R	W
D Govindraj	10	2	39	0	9	2	37	0
E Solkar	12	1	37	1	9	2	15	0
S Gavaskar	3	0	9	0				
S Venkataraghavan	17	1	94	0	15	3	53	0
B Chandrasekhar	16	3	59	1	15	3	44	1
B Bedi	16	3	77	0	10	0	44	2
A Mankad	5	1	28	0				

INDIANS	FIRST INNINGS		SECOND INNINGS	
A Mankad	not out	154	c Parfitt b Close	30
K Jayantilal	b Parfitt	8		
S Gavaskar	c Lewis b Hobbs	2	b Hobbs	128
G Viswanath	c Walker b Parfitt	3	c sub b Hobbs	21
A Ali Baig	c Close b Hobbs	22	b Hobbs	33
E Solkar	c Virgin b Walker	79	not out	7
S Venkataraghavan(c)	c Price b Hobbs	5	c sub b Hobbs	16
D Govindraj	c Price b Hobbs	12	not out	8
P Krishnamurthy†	st Taylor b Hobbs	5		
B Bedi	c Hobbs b Boyce	4		
B Chandrasekhar	b Boyce	0		
Extras	(b 1, lb 3, nb 8)	12	(b 2, lb 3, nb 4)	9
Team score		306		252/5

Fall of wickets 1st innings: 1-35, 2-38, 3-45, 4-91, 5-214, 6-244, 7-276, 8-289, 9-306, 10-306

Fall of wickets 2nd innings: 1-68, 2-185, 3-211, 4-222, 5-240

Bowling figures	O	M	R	W	O	M	R	W
J Price	14	2	44	0	6	0	13	0
K Boyce	13.4	3	33	2	8	0	39	0
P Parfitt	22	8	59	2	13	2	53	0
R Hobbs	32	4	94	5	17.5	3	64	4
P Walker	16	2	64	1	10	0	38	0
B Close					7	2	36	1

India Tour of England
1971 – Statistics

By Kaustubh Gudipati

First-Class batting and fielding record of Indians

Player	M	I	R	NO	AVG	H	F	HS	CT	ST
F Engineer	4	7	262	2	52.40	0	2	62*	8	1
E Solkar	16	24	802	6	44.55	1	6	113	14	0
S Gavaskar	15	27	1,141	1	43.88	3	6	194	15	0
A Mankad	13	22	795	3	41.84	2	4	154*	8	0
G Viswanath	16	27	946	4	41.13	3	5	122	4	0
A Wadekar	16	27	1,057	1	40.65	2	6	150	23	0
S Abid Ali	14	21	552	4	32.47	1	2	102*	11	0
A Baig	13	21	526	0	25.04	0	2	64	6	0
S Kirmani	7	9	118	4	23.60	0	0	37*	7	0
D Sardesai	15	25	495	4	23.57	1	3	120	5	0
D Govindraj	12	16	172	7	19.11	0	0	40*	5	0
K Jayantilal	10	15	237	1	16.92	0	2	84	7	0
S Venkataraghavan	14	21	303	1	15.15	0	1	57	12	0
E Prasanna	9	7	33	3	8.25	0	0	10*	1	0
P Krishnamurthy	9	9	56	2	8.00	0	0	32	16	8
B Bedi	13	14	50	6	6.25	0	0	8	5	0
B Chandrasekhar	13	10	16	4	2.66	0	0	6	9	0

First-Class bowling record of Indians

Player	I	O	M	W	AVG	FW	TW	BBI	BBM
B Chandrasekhar	25	472.5	103	50	24.86	5	1	6/34	11/127
S Venkataraghavan	27	594.2	137	63	24.90	2	1	9/93	10/169
B Bedi	24	603.5	171	58	25.63	4	0	7/111	9/82
E Prasanna	15	363.3	93	26	33.80	1	0	5/137	5/137
S Gavaskar	14	46.3	5	4	47.50	0	0	2/8	2/33
E Solkar	27	238	46	14	49.42	0	0	3/28	3/38
S Abid Ali	27	303.5	53	16	57.87	0	0	4/64	4/90
A Mankad	8	30	6	2	61.00	0	0	1/8	1/8
D Govindraj	22	203	46	11	61.27	0	0	2/37	4/111
S Kirmani	1	2	0	0	-	0	0	-	-
D Sardesai	2	5	0	0	-	0	0	-	-
K Jayantilal	1	5	0	0	-	0	0	-	-
A Baig	1	4	0	0	-	0	0	-	-
A Wadekar	3	10	2	0	-	0	0	-	-

Test batting record of India

Player	M	I	R	NO	AVG	F	HS
F Engineer	3	5	172	1	43.00	1	59
E Solkar	3	5	168	1	42.00	2	67
A Wadekar	3	6	204	0	34.00	1	85
D Sardesai	3	6	147	1	29.40	1	54
G Viswanath	3	6	128	1	25.60	1	68
S Gavaskar	3	6	144	0	24.00	2	57
S Venkataraghavan	3	4	62	0	15.50	0	24
S Abid Ali	3	5	50	1	12.50	0	26
A Mankad	3	6	42	0	7.00	0	11
B Bedi	3	4	12	1	4.00	0	8
B Chandrasekhar	3	3	4	3	-	0	4*

Test bowling record of India

Player	M	I	O	M	W	AVG	FW	BBI
E Solkar	3	6	58.0	16	6	22.83	0	3/28
S Venkataraghavan	3	6	150.3	38	13	26.92	0	4/52
B Chandrasekhar	3	6	146.1	32	13	29.15	1	6/38
B Bedi	3	6	151.3	46	11	29.54	0	4/70
S Abid Ali	3	6	97.4	14	5	53.80	0	4/64
S Gavaskar	3	3	15.0	3	0	-	0	-

Test batting record of England

Player	M	I	R	NO	AVG	H	F	HS
A Knott	3	5	223	0	44.60	0	2	90
B Luckhurst	3	6	244	0	40.66	1	1	101
J Jameson	2	4	141	0	35.25	0	1	82
R Illingworth	3	5	175	0	35.00	1	0	107
R Hutton	3	5	129	1	32.25	0	1	81
J Edrich	3	6	180	0	30.00	0	2	62
J Snow	2	4	85	0	21.25	0	1	73
G Boycott	1	2	36	0	18.00	0	0	33
B D'Oliveira	3	6	88	1	17.60	0	0	30
D Underwood	1	2	33	0	16.50	0	0	22
N Gifford	2	3	32	1	16.00	0	0	17
K Fletcher	2	4	30	1	10.00	0	0	28*
D Amiss	1	2	9	0	4.50	0	0	9
J Price	3	5	9	2	3.00	0	0	5*
P Lever	1	1	88	1	-	0	1	88*

Test bowling record of England

Player	M	I	O	M	W	AVG	FW	BBI
B Luckhurst	3	1	2.0	0	1	9.00	0	1/9
N Gifford	2	2	64.3	18	8	15.87	0	4/43
P Lever	1	2	33.0	7	5	16.80	1	5/70
J Price	3	6	81.0	21	8	25.87	0	2/30
B D'Oliveira	3	5	58.0	28	3	27.66	0	2/40
J Snow	2	4	74.0	21	6	28.16	0	2/64
R Illingworth	3	5	118.3	43	7	28.85	1	5/70
D Underwood	1	2	63.0	20	4	30.25	0	3/72
R Hutton	3	5	60.0	14	4	32.75	0	2/38

Key: M – Matches, I – Innings, R – Runs, Avg – Average, HS – Highest Score, H – Hundreds, F – Fifties, NO – Not Outs, O – Overs, W – Wickets, FW – Five Wickets, TW – Ten Wickets, BBI – Innings Best Bowling.

Air India Flight Diverted to Delhi to Facilitate Meeting With Indira Gandhi

The year 1971 was pivotal in more than cricketing ways for India. While Ajit Wadekar and his men inspired the nation with their wins in West Indies and England, Prime Minister Indira Gandhi took a firm stand with Pakistan on the Bangladeshi liberation struggle. By the end of the year, Bangladesh was born and India's victory in that conflict with their neighbours is still remembered as one of its most defining moments. When Wadekar's team won the Test match at The Oval, there was a congratulatory call from the Prime Minister's Office.

When Wadekar and his men got ready to head back home, they were told that their Air India flight was specially diverted to Delhi. This was unlike April, where they had flown back to Bombay directly. This time, the Prime Minister wanted to meet the team and congratulate them on a special achievement. "Palam Airport was decorated with festoons and banners," said Wadekar. There were also a few dancers performing the Bhangra to welcome the team[119].

---

119 My Cricketing Years, Ajit Wadekar as told to KN Prabhu, p. 123. Published by Vikas Publishing House Pvt Ltd 1973

A felicitation with numerous dignitaries was then held at the Feroz Shah Kotla. There was a lot of talk about India being the "world champions" having vanquished England in their own den. However, captain Wadekar was cautious and announced that "We are yet to beat Australia.[120]"

The following day, the team departed for Mumbai, where the festivities continued.

120 Sunder Rajan, India vs England 1971, Published by Jaico Publishing House. Second Impression 1972. P. 107

Victorious Team Gets Motorcade in Bombay

"I know the board does not have a long enough carpet but if the Government of India or Maharashtra can organise it, let it stretch from Santa Cruz to CCI," said Mansur Ali Khan Pataudi, hailing the Indian team's achievement in England[121]. Pataudi's suggestion was taken in spirit as a carpet of warmth, appreciation and fanfare was laid out along the said path.

If the players were moved by the scenes at the Bombay airport in April 1971 following their victory in the West Indies, it went a notch higher when they returned from England. The short trip to Delhi to meet the Prime Minister was only the beginning! When the team landed in Bombay, the festivities started from the tarmac.

"It all started as we left the flight," Kenia Jayantilal recalls. People had come forward to receive them at the tarmac. "We were told not to worry about our luggage and that it would be delivered to us," Jayantilal said as the Indian team went along with the festivities[122].

---

121 Khalid A-H Ansari – Interview with Mansur Ali Khan Pataudi. Sportsweek, September 5, 1971, p. 5
122 Conversation with the author

An open-roof motorcade was organised through the streets of Bombay. Thousands of people had gathered along the streets as Wadekar and his men waved back at them to acknowledge all the fanfare. "What was most touching was that it was so spontaneous. People lined the streets and cheered. Rose petals were showered on us as we passed through Shivaji Park and Girgaum. I remember spotting Nandu Natekar (former badminton champion) somewhere cheering in the crowd," Wadekar said[123].

Wadekar and his men were felicitated at the Brabourne Stadium, which was then the unofficial home of Indian cricket. Once the celebrations were done, the players quietly retired to their homes or their accommodation. Wadekar took a taxi back home.

Fast forward to 2007, these scenes were replicated when Mahendra Singh Dhoni and his men lifted the inaugural ICC World T20 in South Africa – an event that created a major shift in world cricket. A city that never sleeps had been brought to a standstill by a group of young men 36 years apart!

123 Satish Nandgaonkar, Then in cricket artery, now in Mumbai heart - 1971-2007: Tale of two victory parades'. The Telegraph. Published on September 25, 2007. Accessed at: https://www.telegraphindia.com/india/then-in-cricket-artery-now-in-mumbai-heart-1971-2007-tale-of-two-victory-parades/cid/682293

The Men Who Made History

AJIT WADEKAR

A late-bloomer, the left-handed Ajit Wadekar took to cricket seriously only while he was in college and rose through the ranks to break into the strong Bombay side. At the age of 25, he made his Test debut at his home ground, the Brabourne Stadium, in 1966-67 against the visiting West Indians. While Wadekar only finished with a solitary Test century and an average of 31.07, he is best remembered for leading India to its twin successes in the West Indies and England in 1971. In 1972-73, he led India to another series-win over England, this time on home soil. However, his international career ended following India's forgettable tour to England in 1974, which featured the ignominy of being bowled out for 42 at Lord's and surrender the series 3-0. On that tour, he also became India's first captain in One-Day Internationals (ODIs), scoring 67 on debut.

In the early 1990s, Wadekar took over as the manager-cum-coach of the Indian team – forging a partnership with captain Mohammad Azharuddin. While India had a few successes, his tenure ended with a heart-breaking semi-final exit from the 1996 World Cup at home. His time at the helm coincided with the rise of Sachin Tendulkar – when he was promoted to open the batting in ODIs. In later years, he also served as chairman of selectors. Wadekar passed away in 2018 at the age of 77 in Mumbai.

S VENKATARAGHAVAN

There aren't many men in cricket like Srinivas Venkataraghavan. Across a long cricketing journey, he has donned numerous hats – having been a player, captain, manager, administrator and umpire. A part of the famous spin quartet – this off-spinner was a different bowler when compared to his colleagues – bowling faster and relying on accuracy. However, to add to his cricketing repertoire, he was more than a capable batsman and a good fielder. Ahead of the twin tours in 1971, he was named Wadekar's deputy. His most notable performance that year came during the victory at Port-of-Spain, Trinidad, where his five-wicket haul helped limit the West Indies in the second innings. During India's crucial draw in the fifth Test at Trinidad, he contributed with an important half-century in the first innings.

Venkataraghavan held the distinction of captaining India in the first two World Cups – 1975 and 1979 in England. In all, he represented India in 57 Tests and 15 ODIs. In terms of length, he boasts of one of the longest international careers having started his journey in 1965 against New Zealand and bowing out in 1983.

In later years, Venkataraghavan became a popular face amongst the fans as an umpire – with a distinct style of giving a batsman out with his hand outstretched on the side. Venkataraghavan was also the first Indian to make it to ICC's Elite Panel of Umpires, adding a further 73 Tests and 52 ODIs to his appearances at the highest level.

SUNIL GAVASKAR

Arguably India's greatest Test batsman, Sunil Gavaskar's name is etched in the annals of the game's history. The first man to score 10,000 Test runs, the right-handed opener was the epitome of technique, talent and concentration. Having announced himself with 774 runs in his very first series against the West Indies in

1971, Gavaskar's star continued to rise through the 1970s and by the 1980s, he had etched his name in Test cricket's record books. His 34 Test centuries remained a record until he was overtaken by his natural successor, Sachin Tendulkar. Gavaskar was also a part of India's 1983 World Cup-winning side.

Gavaskar captained India, with his most notable success coming in 1985, when they won the Benson and Hedges World Series in Australia. He bowed out of Test cricket in 1987 with a characteristic 96 against arch-rivals Pakistan on a crumbling pitch at Bangalore. Later in the year, he hit his first one-day century against New Zealand at Nagpur and brought curtains to his international career following India's semi-final exit during the World Cup at home.

Post-retirement, Gavaskar has been a respected media personality and a regular in the commentary box. Wearing an administrator's hat, he served on the International Cricket Council's (ICC) Cricket Committee. In 2014, he was asked by the Supreme Court of India to serve as an interim president of the Board of Control for Cricket in India (BCCI). Gavaskar's son Rohan also represented India in ODIs.

DILIP SARDESAI

Nicknamed the "Renaissance Man" for his feats in the Caribbean in 1971, Dilip Sardesai kick-started India's cricketing revolution with numerous rescue acts that year. Born in Goa, then a Portuguese-ruled colony, Sardesai came to Bombay as a teenager and took to the game. While he was one of the pillars that formed the strong Bombay line-up in the 1960s, he wasn't a fixture in the Indian team. In 1962, he opened the batting in the Caribbean, a tour during which the West Indies pace battery shattered India's morale. This after the Indian captain Nari Contractor was put out of action by Charlie Griffith. Prior to 1971, his two Test centuries had come in back-to-back matches against New Zealand in 1965, with one of them being a double at Brabourne Stadium.

In 1971, Sardesai was drafted into the Indian side at the insistence of the newly appointed captain Wadekar. The captain's faith was repaid in a mountain of runs as Sardesai rescued India with a double century in the first Test and an important 150 in the fourth at Barbados. In the second Test at Trinidad, his 112 set the foundation for India's win. Gavaskar's monumental tally may have outshined Sardesai's but no one can deny the importance of his 642 runs in the Test series in the West Indies. While he wasn't as big a success on the tour to England, his crucial 40 at The Oval helped India during a nervy run-chase on the final day.

Sardesai played his last Test against the visiting Englishmen in 1972. He died in Mumbai in 2007. Instituted in his memory, the Dilip Sardesai Award is presented to the best Indian performer in a Test series against the West Indies. The Dilip Sardesai Memorial Lecture is held every year in Mumbai, where a prominent cricketing figure is invited to deliver the address.

BISHAN SINGH BEDI

A classical left-arm spinner, Bishan Singh Bedi was a purist's dream. The words "poetry in motion" couldn't be used in a better cricketing context than to describe Bedi's left-arm orthodox action. The lovely loop and the ability to flight the ball made him one of the best spinners in the world. By the time he finished, he was India's leading wicket-taker in Tests with 266 scalps in 67 matches. In First-Class cricket, his tally of 1560 wickets is the most for an Indian bowler. In the mid-1970s, he captained India, a tenure that included a hard-fought tour to Australia in 1977-78 and a few controversial brushes with the authorities and the opposition. His international career ended following the tour to England in 1979.

Post retirement, Bedi was one of the selectors that picked India's World Cup-winning side in 1983. In the 1990s, he was also appointed manager of the Indian team for a brief period. He has dabbled in coaching from time to time, most notably taking charge of Jammu and Kashmir. Known to express his opinion without inhibitions, Bedi has found himself in a controversy after another owing to his typical no-holds-barred comments. A purist in every sense, he has made no secret of his disdain for modern-day T20 and is an outspoken critic of suspected bowling actions.

ERAPALLI PRASANNA

A crafty off-spinner who was hailed for his tricks, Erapalli Prasanna was in the classical mould. Ian Chappell called him the best spinner he faced. "He was seeking your wicket every ball that he bowled and you knew you were locked in a serious mental battle each time you faced him," he said[124]. Hailing from Bangalore, Prasanna made his Test debut as a 21-year-old during the home series against England in 1961-62. However, two Tests in, he took a break to complete his engineering degree. In 1967, he made a comeback to the Indian team at a time when Mansur Ali Khan Pataudi went about building the spin quartet. His main rival being S Venkataraghavan, Prasanna's guile won over during selection but the former's superior batting and fielding skills kept him in the hunt. He was a part of both tours in 1971 but did not play a Test in England.

In 1976, Prasanna took eight for 76 against New Zealand at Auckland, which remain the best figures by an Indian bowler overseas. His international career finished after the tour to Pakistan in 1978. With close to a thousand wickets in First-Class cricket, he was a stalwart for Karnataka/Mysore – having captained them to two Ranji Trophy victories.

---

124 Fortune Turners

Prasanna served as manager of the Indian team that lifted the 1985 Benson and Hedges World Championship of Cricket in Australia under the captaincy of Gavaskar.

BHAGWAT CHANDRASEKHAR

Bhagwat Chandrasekhar stood out from the pack for he was the most unorthodox with his fastish leg-spin. Behind this game-changer is a story that tugs the heart and reflects a character that has overcome great odds. Despite suffering from polio in childhood – which weakened his arm, Chandrasekhar worked his way to become a leg-spin bowler. Having made his debut against England in 1964, he then became an integral part of MAK Pataudi's Indian team that built itself around spinners. However, in 1967-68, he picked up an injury in Australia. A motorcycle accident further kept him out of the game. Chandrasekhar only returned to Test cricket after more than three years.

In 1971, he wasn't picked for the tour to the West Indies but returned for the England series. Vijay Merchant believed it was a gamble, but it paid off when Chandrasekhar delivered with that historic six-wicket haul to help win The Oval Test. The following year, he recorded his Test best of eight for 79 against the visiting Englishmen. His six for 94 at Auckland in 1976 helped set the stage for India's win against New Zealand. At Melbourne in 1977-78, he bagged identical figures of six for 52 in each innings to help setup another victory. These impact performances truly reveal the importance of Chandra.

One of the game's genuine No. 11s, Chandrasekhar finished with 167 Test runs as opposed to 242 wickets.

GUNDAPPA VISWANATH

If Sunil Gavaskar was India's lynchpin at the top, Gundappa Viswanath was its dependable artist in the middle-order. One of the most elegant batsmen, Viswanath was known to mesmerise the crowds with his wristy stroke-play, with the flicks and cuts forming his armoury against bowlers. Hailing from Karnataka, he announced himself with a century on debut against Bill Lawry's Australians in 1969. In the 1970s, he formed a vital part of India's batting line-up, scripting numerous dependable and rescue acts. One of his best performances came against the West Indies in 1974-75 at Chennai where his artistry took on the might of Andy Roberts and Co to score 97. An innings of 112 helped India overhaul a mammoth target of 403 at Trinidad in 1976. In 1981, his first innings century against Australia at Melbourne laid the groundwork for what turned out to be an unexpected Indian win. A career-best of 222 also came at Chennai in 1982 against England. Whenever Viswanath scored a Test century, India never lost. He last played for India on their tour to Pakistan in 1982-83.

Viswanath later served as chairman of selectors in the mid 1990s. He then took on the mantle of being an ICC Match Referee, officiating in 15 Tests and 78 ODIs.

SYED ABID ALI

A Hyderabadi all-rounder, S Abid Ali announced himself with a six-wicket haul on Test debut at Adelaide against Australia in 1967. A handy player, Abid was also a capable batsman and a good fielder. In 1971, he became the first Indian bowler to take a wicket off the first ball in Test cricket when he dismissed Roy Fredericks at Trinidad in the second Test. A team-man, when asked to open the batting, he took up the challenge. As a bowler, his main role was to take the shine off the ball for the spinners but invariably chipped in when needed. He was the common factor when the winning runs were hit at both Trinidad and The Oval in 1971 – although he handed those duties to Gavaskar in the first.

Abid last played for India at the 1975 World Cup. Considering the way one-day cricket evolved, Abid may have been an ideal player for the format. Post retirement, he went on to coach numerous teams including the United Arab Emirates. He now lives in California, USA.

EKNATH SOLKAR

Arguably India's greatest fielder at short-leg, Eknath Solkar's quick reflexes were worth their weight in gold. A captain's cricketer, Solkar would do what was demanded by the team. As a batsman, he could score vital runs down the order but also batted at the top when required – getting his only Test century at No. 3 against the West Indies in 1974-75. While his medium-pace was mainly used to take the shine off the ball before the spinners came into force, he could be more than useful – ask Geoffrey Boycott! However, Solkar is remembered for some blinders he took at short-leg off the spinners, especially at critical times in 1971. He featured in 27 Tests and seven ODIs until 1977.

Solkar died in 2005 at the age of 57 after an illness. A popular personality in the dressing room, he is missed by all his teammates.

KENIA JAYANTILAL

A lot was expected of Hyderabad's Kenia Jayantilal when he boarded the flight to the Caribbean in 1971. However, the Hyderabadi was unfortunate to get only the solitary Test match in Jamaica, where his lone innings ended thanks to a brilliant catch by Garry Sobers. Sunil Gavaskar played the next Test and never looked back! Jayantilal scored runs in the tour games but couldn't break into the playing XI. He also made the trip to England and took an important catch in the second innings at The Oval as a substitute. Thereafter, he wasn't picked for India again, despite getting a century against the touring Englishmen for South Zone in 1972-73.

Jayantilal played for Hyderabad until the late 1970s before moving to Mumbai. In retirement, he has dabbled in cricket coaching.

ASHOK MANKAD

The son of the legendary Vinoo Mankad, Ashok was one of the big names in the strong Bombay team of the 1960s and 70s. A middle-order batsman, he made his international debut during the home season in 1969-70 and scored a crucial 97 in a Test against Australia. In 1971, Ashok was tasked with the responsibility of opening the batting with Gavaskar. While he made fighting contributions in the West Indies, his form fell-away in the Tests in England. It was bizarre as he kept getting the runs in tour matches but couldn't produce the same in the three Tests. He was dropped from the Indian team after the 1971 tour and only returned in 1974, during a forgettable visit to England. He played his last Test in Australia in 1977-78.

In later years, Ashok was a respected coach in the domestic circles. Nicknamed 'Kaka', he was popular for his wit and sense of humour. The Mankads are a true sporting family. He married tennis player Nirupama and their son Harsh also represented India in the Davis Cup. In 2008, Ashok passed away in Mumbai.

FAROKH ENGINEER

A dashing wicket-keeper batsman, Farokh Engineer's flamboyant personality reflected in his game. At the time of writing, he is the last Parsee man to play Test cricket for India. Having made his debut in 1961, he competed with Budhi Kunderan for the gloves early in his career. By the late 1960s, Engineer firmly established himself as the first choice. As a batsman, he was dashing and trusted to score quick runs. Against the West Indies in 1966-67, he smashed 94 before lunch on Day One while opening the batting. In 1971, he wasn't picked for the tour to the West Indies due to the board's policy disqualifying players who didn't appear in the previous domestic season. By then, Engineer had taken up a contract with Lancashire and settled down in England with family. However, he was called up for the England tour and played his part in the subsequent triumph. Engineer played for India until 1975, featuring in the first ever World Cup. He continues to live in England and has tried his hand at commentary post retirement.

P KRISHNAMURTHY

A wicketkeeper from Hyderabad, P Krishnamurthy was selected for the twin tours in 1971. He 'kept in all the five Tests in West Indies but never played for India thereafter. Farokh Engineer's return to the side in England sidelined him to the bench for the Test matches. In 1976, he made a comeback to the Indian team for the tour to New Zealand and featured in an ODI. Krishnamurthy died at the relatively young age of 51 in 1999.

ML JAISIMHA

ML Jaisimha is best remembered for smashing 74 and 101 at Brisbane in 1968, having stepped out of a flight hours before a Test match. One of the glam boys of Indian cricket in the 1960s, the stylish Jaisimha emerged from the Hyderabad school of batting and made his Test debut at Lord's in 1959. While his international record doesn't reflect the true quality of his batsmanship, he remained a big name in domestic cricket. In 39 Tests, he finished with 2,056 runs at an average of 30.68 and three centuries. In 1971, he was called out of wilderness as one of the senior batsmen to tour West Indies. He wasn't among the runs but his tactical contributions were of immense help to the new captain Wadekar. He also left a huge impression on a young Gavaskar.

Post retirement, Jaisimha served as the manager of the Indian team on a tour and also made a name as a commentator. He died at the age of 60 in 1999.

SALIM DURANI

Nicknamed "Prince" by a few, Salim Durani was an enigmatic and mercurial figure in Indian cricket. On his day, his flamboyance stole the show for being a true game-changer. A left-arm spinner and a batsman, Durani could be a captain's trump-card in a game. A tally of 29 Tests over a 13-year career doesn't do justice to his enormous talents but he left behind many memories. In the early 1960s, his bowling came into prominence during the home series-win against England, where he formed a good spin-bowling partnership with Chandu Borde. A brave century batting at No. 3 at Trinidad showcased his natural batting ability. However, it was in 1971, where he left his biggest impact on Indian cricket – a small but decisive contribution to the country's history. Brought in to bowl during a crucial moment at Trinidad in the second Test, he delivered with wickets of Garry Sobers and Clive Lloyd to put India firmly in command of the game.

Durani was dropped after a largely indifferent West Indies tour and only returned during the home series against England the following year in 1972-73. He bowed out of Test cricket at the Brabourne Stadium but not before he had earned a reputation of hitting sixes on the crowd's demands.

Off the field, Durani featured in a Hindi movie titled *Charitra* alongside Parveen Babi. He now lives in Jamnagar, Gujarat

RUSI JEEJEEBHOY

A surprise selection for the tour to the West Indies in 1971, Rusi Jeejeebhoy was a wicketkeeper for Bengal in domestic cricket. Jeejeebhoy 'kept wickets in the Duleep Trophy final ahead of the selection meeting in early 1971 and was given the nod by the selectors. Jeejeebhoy was dropped after the West Indies tour and wasn't considered again. He played 46 First-Class matches during his career.

SYED KIRMANI

Syed Kirmani is one of the finest wicketkeepers India has produced. Although he was picked for the tour to England in 1971, he had to wait until the retirement of Farokh Engineer to make his international debut. Kirmani eventually donned the Test cap in 1976 and established himself with his solid wicketkeeping – featuring in 88 Test matches. A part of the 1983 World Cup winning side, he won the Best Wicketkeeper of the Tournament Award, handed to him by Godfrey Evans. With 198 dismissals in Tests, he was India's most successful wicketkeeper until MS Dhoni broke his record. A useful batsman, he also scored two Test centuries and 12 fifties. One of those centuries came as a night-watchman against Australia in 1979. While his international career ended in 1986, Kirmani kept featuring in domestic cricket for Karnataka well into his 40s and called it a day in 1994.

D GOVINDRAJ

D Govindraj, the Hyderabad player, was the only quick bowler India took to the West Indies and England. Despite featuring in the tour matches, he did not make it into the Test side and was discarded after the two sojourns. Govindraj was a regular for Hyderabad for years before breaking into the Indian side. In 93 First-Class appearances until 1974-75, he took 190 wickets at an average of 27.66. Post retirement from cricket, he moved to England to work with the State Bank of India (SBI). He now lives in Hyderabad and dabbles in coaching.

ABBAS ALI BAIG

In 1959, Abbas Ali Baig was drafted into the Indian team while still a student at Oxford University. Making his Test debut at Manchester, he scored a century in the second innings against an attack led by Fred Trueman. At the age of 20, many would have expected a long career but Baig ended up playing only 10 Tests

248 | Twice upon a Time

across seven years and only scored two fifties after his heroics on debut. Baig was called up for the England sojourn in 1971 but had an unsuccessful time in the tour games and did not feature in any of the Test matches. He ended his First-Class career with 235 matches and over 12,000 runs, representing Hyderabad in domestic cricket with distinction.